THRIFTY TIPS

FROM THE

WAR YEARS

THRIFTY TIPS
—————FROM THE—————
WAR YEARS

JANICE ANDERSON

Futura

FUTURA

First published in Great Britain in 2010 by Futura

A CIP catalogue record for this book
is available from the British Library.

ISBN 978-0-7088-6528-6

Typeset in Great Britain by Omnipress Limited
Printed and bound in China

Futura
An imprint of
Little, Brown Book Group
100 Victoria Embankment
London EC4Y 0DY

An Hachette UK Company
www.hachette.co.uk

www.littlebrown.co.uk

Photo credits: Getty Images

CONTENTS

INTRODUCTION

Although we cannot fully realise the hardships that people endured during World War Two, the current economic crisis has meant that many people have had to tighten their belts. Learning ways of saving money and making do with what we have can only be a good thing, so why not try to replicate some of the money-saving measures that our predecessors practised to make life more comfortable.

During the war years nearly everything was rationed – food, clothes, fuel and household goods – but people managed and learned not to complain. The modern generation has got so used to having luxuries that when a piece of equipment breaks down, they find it difficult to cope without it. Mobile phones, computers, washing machines, televisions and refrigerators are just a few of the things we take for granted, and I imagine it is difficult for you conceive your life without any one of these.

Our ancestors not only coped, they managed extremely well and did everything they could to help the war effort and – in turn – their country. Everything possible was recycled, salvaged, or repaired and what people didn't have they didn't miss. Today we are being taught to recycle for different reasons – to save our planet – so a few tips on how to be more economical and how to be aware of the pollution we are causing could benefit not just your household but the entire world.

People who lived through the war learned to live by certain codes:

- Keep Calm and Carry On

- Make Do and Mend

- Always Walk When You Can

- Save Fuel for War

- Save Kitchen Scraps to Feed the Pigs

- Don't Waste a Drop of Water

- Save Waste Paper

- Dig for Victory

- Holiday at Home

- Eat to Keep Healthy

Living by these simple rules meant that everyone pulled together and that they were playing their part towards winning the war. They may have looked a little tired, bedraggled and somewhat dreary, but they were warmly clothed, well-fed on the whole and had shoes on their feet. How did they do it? Careful planning and living by the motto 'Make Do and Mend' and, of course, never giving up. For many the war years were spent in relative security of the countryside after being evacuated out of London. Thousands of children boarded trains for the unknown, carrying just a few possessions. It was frightening and bewildering, but it was for their own good. For the people who were left behind, many had to witness horrific sights and experience major upheavals especially when they lost loved ones. Life was changing fast and they had to make many adjustments.

People had to be creative to make sure their houses were made secure so that no light escaped through the windows. Very heavy curtains had to be made to hang at the doors and windows and shutters erected. The windows were often covered with brown adhesive paper or a type of cellophane to stop the glass from shattering. Many nights were spent in air raid shelters to the sound of bombs destroying everything around them.

People learned to barter – if you had a surplus of potatoes you could swap it for half a dozen eggs or some apples. Housewives learned to make some really tasty dishes using the minimum of ingredients. People turned to growing their own food or even raiding the hedgerows to supplement their diets. Rationing was just a part of everyday life and pooling resources was commonplace.

It wasn't just food that was hard to come by, clothing coupons were just as precious. Because clothes were difficult to get hold of, the 'Make Do and Mend' motto was practised by every household. Sheets were turned outside to middle, blankets were turned into warm winter coats, new collars and cuffs were fitted

to worn shirts and wool was reknitted to make school jumpers or vests for children, even if they did itch like mad.

The radio became a pivotal piece of equipment, with people not only relying on it for news of the war but for their only source of entertainment. *ITMA – It's That Man Again –* was very much a part of the war scene with Tommy Handley playing a succession of strange characters from Office of Twerps to the disapproving civil servant Fusspot. Looking back it all seems very uncomplicated, but somehow everyone looked on the bright side of life.

Try working your way through some of the Thrifty Tip boxes and see whether you can change your way of life. Start by doing something each week and gradually build up until it becomes a part of your normal routine. Remember, everything you dispose of can be recycled and used for many different reasons.

LIFE IN BRITAIN IN 1939

On 3 September 1939, the British people found themselves at war for the second time in the twentieth century. They lived in a very different society from the post-Edwardian country whose young men had joined up to fight the 'Boche' so enthusiastically in 1914. They were also about to be plunged into a very different kind of warfare, one which put them on a major war front – the Home Front, as it was soon called – as citizen combatants.

By the end of the 1930s, the hard years of the Depression were beginning to seem a bad memory for most people in Britain. True, in the big cities there were still far too many really poor people – as the nation was to discover when thousands of children and their mothers from cities and industrial areas considered to be in danger of bombing were evacuated to quieter, safer places in September 1939. But for most people, Britain in the late 1930s was a comfortable country to live in.

It had a large middle-class of independent-minded salary earners and a working class, supported by strong trade unions, whose wages were on the rise. The middle and better-off working classes had continued the rapid expansion that had begun in the later years of Queen Victoria's reign. The average worker and his family now lived in a pleasantly designed semi-detached house with its own garden set behind a neat fence in one of the tree-lined streets of the suburbs which were spreading across thousands of acres of what was once farmland and villages on the edges of towns and cities. Across Britain, more than a quarter of all houses were owned by their occupiers – a dramatic change, indeed, from the end of the nineteenth century.

In the average family, the husband and father was the breadwinner. Despite their essential work during World War One, most women still followed the pre-war convention of giving up their jobs – if they had them, and many middle-class women did not work when they married. The average British woman was a housewife, and a good number of middle-class homes, including many of those neat semis in the suburbs, still employed domestic staff.

There were no supermarkets, and the housewife did her shopping in a range of shops in the high street. She was known by name by the butcher, baker, greengrocer and grocer

A GOOD SUPPLY OF MEAT

There were no supermarkets as we know them today, so housewives went from shop to shop to buy their weekly needs. Meat rationing was introduced during the war as the government took control of the nation's slaughter houses. The job of meat allocation was difficult, and Saturday morning queues often stretched down the street and around the corner.

where she shopped several times a week and each trip to the shops was a social occasion. Her shopping was often delivered to her home, either in a van or by a man or a boy on a bike. The working-class housewife also had the local market, where goods were cheaper, but still plentiful.

In most households food was stored in cupboards, larders and pantries. Refrigerators, which were either gas- or electricity-powered, were not yet widely used and if a household did not have one in 1939, it was very unlikely to get even a second-hand one until after the war was over.

A WARTIME ESSENTIAL:
Fuel Economy

Britain's power supplies were coal-based, so the wartime needs of British industry made it absolutely essential for everyone to be thrifty with fuel. As a Ministry of Fuel and Power 'Fuel Communique', inserted in *Good Housekeeping* magazine in 1943, put it:

'Britain's 12,000,000 households are 12,000,000 battle fronts in this great drive to save fuel. Each one counts. Each one must do its part. An *active* part, for it isn't enough to stop wasting coal or gas or electricity or paraffin; there must be *economies* in the use of fuel in all its forms…

'Housewives, you have done splendidly so far – you have put your hearts into this great effort to help the war effort. Colder weather makes the struggle harder for you now – *but keep it up*. Put your wits to work as well as your will-power and plan your own special ways of saving.'

And, advised the Ministry, here's how it could be done:

- Save a fire one or two nights a week by sharing with friends and neighbours.
- Save coal or coke when using the oven or boiler by banking the fire up with slack, this prevents cold air entering.
- Save on your gas fire by not turning it full on; or if you have an electric heater which has two or more bars use only one.
- Save while cooking by using the small gas ring instead of the large one.
- Save hot water by never using more than 5 inches in the bath; and by doing the day's washing-up all at one time.
- Turn your central heating thermostat down a notch or two and put on an extra layer to keep you warm.

The majority of houses in towns and cities were connected to the mains and used electricity for lighting and to power a wide variety of labour-saving domestic gadgets, including irons, vacuum cleaners, electric drills and screwdrivers (the middle-classes, who had learned to be thrifty in the years of the Depression, were becoming adept at do-it-yourself), hairdryers, sewing machines, and electric blankets (sometimes called 'electric bed-warmers').

Gas was still used for lighting in many homes and was the fuel of choice for cookers and for water heating, with only about 25 per cent of houses having electric fires, which were often designed to fit into a fireplace, and even fewer having electric cookers. Most homes still had open fireplaces, because coal was cheap and logs were readily available, and many also had portable oil fires and radiators.

While having gas and electricity readily available in the home made life easier for everyone, it also made them less securely independent as householders: it only needed one bomb dropped from an enemy plane to knock out a whole neighbourhood's gas or electricity supply.

Even more important was the fact that a country at war needed much more fuel than a country at peace. As the Ministry of Fuel and Power reminded the readers of *Good Housekeeping* in 1944, '5lbs of coal saved in one day by 1,500,000 homes will provide enough fuel to build a destroyer. Is YOUR home helping to build a destroyer? Save FUEL for BATTLE!'. Fuel economy and making the most economic use possible of the coal from Britain's coal mines, was the great underlying theme of all the rationing, 'make do and mend' and 'save

STOKING UP THE BOILER
Small coal boilers needed to be constantly stoked to provide enough hot water for the whole family.

and salvage' schemes that dominated life on the Home Front during the war.

Every opportunity was taken to get the fuel-saving message across – adverts in newspapers and magazines, leaflets in local council offices, 'Fuel Flashes' on the BBC's Home Service – and to the man and woman in the street.

Later on in the war, in 1942, in Regent Street in the heart of London, the Ministry of Fuel and Power put on an entry-free exhibition, The Battle

A WAR KITCHEN
Kitchens were basic during the war having the bear essentials. Above is a chef working in the kitchen of the Cabinet War Rooms beneath Whitehall in London, where the staff's meals were prepared.

for Fuel. This exhibition was designed round a working coal-mine, with dummy miners working at the coal face and a real live pit pony eating hay. Once through the coal mine, the visitor was confronted with a large exhibition in which the many ways in which fuel could be saved in wartime were highlighted. Visitor Herbert Brush confided in the diary he kept for Mass Observation that he was a little doubtful

that the exhibition would have the desired effect: 'I think the only thing I learned was that a two-gallon bucket holds about 12lb of coal or 8lb of coke.'

Just as worrying as the fact that Britain was so dependent on coal-based gas and electricity, was that sixty per cent of Britain's food was imported, arriving by sea on the ships of the merchant navies of Britain and many other

BATHROOM BLITZ

Use natural products to clean your bathroom tiles, not only is it healthier for you and your family but it is kinder to the environment:

- Spray straight vinegar onto the tiles and then scrub using a soft, damp sponge. There is no need to rinse the vinegar off as it will quickly evaporate leaving no smell or nasty residue.
- Make up a paste using equal parts water, baking soda and salt. Rub this paste onto the tile with a sponge. When you have finished, simply rinse out the sponge and use it to remove the paste from the tiles. Finally, dip a clean sponge in neat lemon juice and wipe the tile that you have just cleaned to remove any residue and leave your tiles sparkling clean.

countries. Britain was still the Home country for a vast empire whose members annually shipped to it hundreds of thousands of tons of frozen meat, wheat, fruits and vegetables, and sugar for human consumption as well as hundreds of thousands of tons of grain-based animal feed, leather, timber, fuel oil, petrol and much else essential to life in Britain.

As with fuel economy, so with shipping from overseas, there was a second major strand to the need for economies with food: space on ships once filled by food imports now had to be freed up for tanks, aeroplanes, firearms and ammunition,

HEY – MIND ME FEET!
This wire-haired terrier has to jump to avoid his feet being run over by the vacuum cleaner.

FIGHTING THE WAR
WITH WORDS

From the outset, government ministries used words and slogans as a major tool in the work of persuading the people of Britain that everything they did could help or hinder the war effort. The Ministry of Information was soon fighting the Battle of the Atlantic in the pages of women's magazines such as *Good Housekeeping* with slogans like:

- Fight the Battle of the Atlantic in your planning – save, don't spend!

- Fight the Battle of the Atlantic in your cooking – be resourceful, never wasteful!

- Fight the Battle of the Atlantic in your shopping – do without and lend!

mostly from America. Again and again, the publicity for the great Dig for Victory and Grow Your Own campaigns emphasised the fact that every potato, onion or carrot grown at home left space for munitions on ships: 'Use Spades Not Ships – Grow Your Own Food' said a famous wartime poster.

Whether it came from Australia, New Zealand or South America, India or the Far East, or across the Atlantic, the last leg of the journey for all shipping was into the North Atlantic to ports like Liverpool and Glasgow and up the English Channel to Southampton and London. The shipping lanes were most vulnerable to U-boat attack where they were most concentrated – that is, close to home.

This was Britain at the outbreak of war: far from self-sufficient in the essentials of life and with supply lines for everything that came from overseas vulnerable and fragile. Everyone knew that a second war within a generation of the end of the 1914–18 war would have a devastating effect on Britain because of Germany's great fighting strength in the air and at sea.

Life at home changed little in the first weeks of the war, with the expected all-out bombing attack turning out to be a non-event. While it would be some months before the 'man-in-the-street' and the 'woman-in-the-kitchen' became, as Mass Observation put it in a 1942 report into British war production, 'the-man-in-uniform' and 'the-woman-in-the-workshop', or vice-

MEAGRE RATIONS
Men and women collect their coke rations from the South Metropolitan Gas Company's depot at Vauxhall, London when fuel was at a premium.

USE SPADES NOT SHIPS

GROW YOUR OWN FOOD
AND SUPPLY YOUR OWN COOKHOUSE

TOMATOES ON YOUR WINDOWSILL

You don't need a large garden to grow tomatoes, they can be grown outside in pots and containers or even in a windowbox on a sunny windowsill.

- Choose a variety that is easy to grow – the bush cherry varieties are ideal as they do not need their side shoots pinched out.
- Keep tomato seedlings and young plants in as light an area as possible so they don't become leggy.
- Don't over-water – compost should be just moist, not wet.
- Do not feed with tomato food until the first pea-like fruit appears.

versa, life for Britain's merchant navy was very different. Within hours of that quiet September Sunday morning announcement by Prime Minister Neville Chamberlain that Britain was at war again, the Battle of the Atlantic began.

That battle began so quickly that the main heading, in large black capital letters, on the front page of the *News Chronicle* for Monday, 4 September 1939 shouted 'British Liner Torpedoed, Reported Sunk' and '*Athenia* with 1,400 on Board Feared Lost 200 Miles West of Hebrides'. The announcement, 'Britain and France at War with Germany', was in much smaller letters, albeit underlined, at the top of the page. To say the least, the Battle of the Atlantic was a fight for Britain's very survival.

In the first four months of the war, German U-boats sank nearly 200,000 tons of merchant shipping and their precious cargoes every month: figures so bad (though worse ones were to come in 1940) that the Government did not release them in detail.

If Germany had been successful in totally stopping merchant ships from carrying food

YOUNG OR OLD
July 1942: Regardless of age, everyone had a go at growing their own vegetables.

NEVER GIVE UP

May 1941: Despite being wounded, soldiers are still prepared to play their part and can be seen here digging the grounds of a Surrey hospital as part of the Dig For Victory scheme.

PRECIOUS METALS

Many items were rationed during World War Two in an effort to make sure that there would be no lack of certain items for the war effort.

Foods and petrol were rationed, but so were metals that were desperately required for weapons. The propaganda poster above asked people to take their silver coins to the Post Office to be turned into much-needed bullets. In fact any metals that could be melted down and used again were salvaged for the war effort. Old cooking pots, iron railings, empty tins and silver wrapping paper were all considered to be 'precious metals' during World War Two.

and other raw materials to Britain, the outcome of the war could have been very different. It is possible that Britain could have been starved into submission, so the government knew they had to act, and act quickly.

The government's response was to exhort everyone to waste nothing, to grow as much food as possible, and to learn to be frugal in their housekeeping, all in phrases that were to become terribly, depressingly familiar in the years ahead.

In other words – to survive, Britain must be thrifty and the British people must learn the truth in the old saying, 'Waste not, want not'. It took a while for everyone to learn that they were all, to take a few words from one of J. B. Priestley's *Postscripts*, soldier-civilians now, joined together 'in the great battle for the future of our civilisation; … instead of being obscure and tucked away, we're bang in the middle of the world's stage with all the spotlights focused on us'. As it turned out, the major weapons in their hands, the habits of thrift, saving and being careful with fuel, served them very well.

Everyone learned to live by the motto:

Use it up

Wear it out

Make it do

Or do without!

KEEP CALM AND CARRY ON

SAVE YOUR STOCKINGS

Don't throw away your old stockings and tights: they can be used in any number of ways:

- Cut into small pieces and use to stuff cushions or hand-made toys for children.
- Want an extra large rubber band? Cut stocking into thin strips and using two or three wrap it around a bundle of newspapers or magazines.
- Old stockings make a wonderful pad for buffing up a wooden floor to a beautiful shine.
- If you drop a contact lens on the floor, cover your vacuum nozzle with a piece of nylon hose to stop the lens being sucked up into oblivion.

FOOD FOR THE PEOPLE

Everyone in Britain either knew or feared from at least the mid-1930s, and certainly after Prime Minister Chamberlain's Munich Agreement with the German Chancellor, Adolf Hitler, in 1938, that a second great war was inevitable. Everyone also knew that, in the event of war, while the needs of industry in wartime would be paramount, the needs of agriculture would be hardly less so.

So, long before that war became actuality in September 1939, government and people began taking steps to ensure that the country would not be starved into submission by a German blockade of the country's ports allied to an all-out attack on merchant shipping in the Atlantic. Throughout the 1920s and 1930s the British government made, up-dated and revised plans to get the country's industrial and agricultural economy on to an effective and productive war footing as quickly as possible and – just as important – to ensure the maintenance of food supplies for both people and livestock. Just as Britain relied on imports to feed its people, so it relied on heavy imports of feeding stuffs to feed its agricultural livestock.

In 1936 a Food (Defence Plans) Department was set up and the country was divided into fifteen administrative divisions. Within these divisions, every local council was ordered to appoint a food executive officer. National stocks of non-perishable essential foods such as wheat and sugar were set aside and food rationing schemes were planned.

The Agriculture Act of 1937 and associated Land Fertility Scheme began the process of getting land into good order for ploughing and for arable crop production. In 1938, the year of Germany's annexation of Austria as well as the Munich Agreement, the Ministry of Agriculture selected the men who would be chairmen of the war agricultural executive committees it intended setting up in the event of war, and the Ministry of Food started preparing food ration books.

From spring 1939, the Ministry of Agriculture took many bold steps towards ensuring that agriculture would be in good shape when war came, including offering farmers a subsidy of

WOMEN'S WORK

March 1942: While their men were away fighting the war, the job of preparing the land for planting often fell to the women. Here two young women are ploughing a field using a triple (foreground) and a single furrow plough which are hauled by tractors.

COQUET PUDDING
(Sufficient for four people)

½ lb potatoes
1½ oz margarine
1½ oz sugar
2 eggs (or use dried if not available)
½ pint milk
1 tablespoon dried fruit or jam

Cook and mash potatoes with margarine.
Add sugar and eggs, beating well.
Mix in milk and fruit and pour into a
greased pie dish. Bake in a moderate
oven for 30 minutes

AN AGRICULTURAL REVOLUTION

During the Second World War, British agriculture, which had been brought to a parlous state during the Depression, virtually turned its production figures upside-down as it became a vitally important source of food. Between 1939 and 1944, roughly six million acres of grassland were turned into arable land, so that the farmland under arable cultivation increased from twelve to eighteen million acres.

The food production figures behind this transformation were very clear: 10 acres of medium grassland used for stock-raising could feed 12 people; convert those 10 acres of land to arable and grow wheat on it, and you would feed 200 people. Grow potatoes on it and you could feed 400 people. In terms of calories provided – and that was the essential figure in wartime – there was no contest: meat, eggs and milk, all of which required large amounts of grazing land in their production, would have to become very carefully rationed in wartime.

And it wasn't just former farm grazing land that was turned over to arable farming. In a splendid extension of the 'waste not, want not' spirit, King George VI turned Windsor Great Park into a small prairie of wheat, an example that was copied by many other owners of large parks. Hundreds of acres of countryside that had never been farmed, including the Sussex Downs (*below*), were also turned over to wheat.

Potatoes and wheat were among the most important crops harvested in Britain during the war, with oats, beans, peas, rye or mixed corn also on the first lists of 'approved crops' that farmers could receive subsidies for growing on newly ploughed acres. Sugar beet (to replace the cane sugar from the West Indies that had long been the country's main source of sugar) also became an important farm crop.

WINDSOR GREAT PARK

July 1942: King George VI inspects the pigs which were kept at Windsor Great Park during the war.

£2 an acre on grassland of at least seven year's standing that was ploughed and cropped, and guaranteeing a market for increased tractor manufacture. By September 1939, Britain's farmers were well on their way towards turning much of the country's grassland over to arable farming.

At the same time, householders were also being put on a war-footing. In spring they were reassured by the President of the Board of Trade that getting in a week's supply of non-perishable foods should be regarded, not as hoarding, but as their patriotic duty. A leaflet produced by the Canned Foods Advisory

PRIME ARABLE LAND
Many of the RAF airfields took over prime arable land, as they needed thick grass to take the weight of the planes. This picture was taken in 1946 as part of a Battle of Britain re-enactment for a television broadcast.

Service early in 1939 suggested that, as well as good stocks of canned foods, housewives should be thinking about getting in stocks of such things as flour, cereals, pulses, tea, coffee, cocoa, sugar and dried fruits and storing them in metal containers with tight-fitting lids.

By the time war eventually happened, most households had good supplies of food in their larders and pantries.

Although farming was a reserved occupation throughout the war, many workers had left the land for better-paid work in industry in the

1920s and 1930s and continued to do so during the war. How could a seventeen-year-old be expected to work as a farm labourer for 20/- (twenty shillings, or £1) a week when he could earn 85/- a week as a carpenter's mate in one of the military camps that were being set up all over the Salisbury Plain, or a shepherd to make do with 35/- (£1.75p) when there was more than twice that on offer for waiters in the mess at the nearby RAF camp?

Incidentally, RAF sites wrested more than labourers from harassed wartime farmers. They also took some of their best arable land. When farmers asked why wouldn't poor land do, they were told that the speed with which new airfields had to be built meant that they had to have land that would very quickly produce a good thick sole of grass to carry aircraft the size of heavy bombers.

The demands of wartime agriculture created a desperate need for agricultural workers. They came with remarkable speed from many sources. Several months before war was actually declared, the government revived World War One's Women's Land Army in June 1939. Where the housewife in the kitchen became the war's woman in the factory, many girls in offices became Land Girls, working down on the farm.

At its peak during the war, the Women's Land Army and its associated Timber Corps employed more than 80,000 women. The majority of Land Girls worked in arable farming, learning to plough, sow and harvest, dig drainage ditches, and even catch rats. But about a quarter of them worked in dairy farming, especially in the milking parlour.

Land Girls often found themselves working side-by-side with pensioners, over 700,000 of

TIMBER!
Landgirls of the Timber Corps fell a tree in a forest near Bury St Edmunds.

whom were recalled into active work during the war, many of them into agriculture, and with German or Italian prisoners of war. At harvest-time farmers were helped to get in the harvest by an army of temporary workers, including servicemen on leave, schoolchildren

We live in a throwaway age where one third of all food bought is actually put in the bin. Take a tip from the war years and learn to reuse your leftovers rather than scooping them into the bin.

- Use up cooked potatoes and vegetables by making bubble and squeak.
- Make bread and butter pudding with stale bread.
- Make soup out of a chicken carcass.
- Make shepherds pie or cottage pie out of the Sunday roast leftovers.
- Use your teabags more than once.
- Leftover roast potatoes can be sliced and turned into a delicious tortilla-style omelette.

on holiday, happy to earn as many sixpences an hour as possible, and platoons of Boy Scouts: a true national effort.

Once American GIs were in Britain in large numbers, many of them helped out at harvest time, too, usually bringing their own transport to move what they had helped to harvest. They did not want cash in return for their work – just hot baths, plus maybe some apples and milk for their camp canteen.

While the contribution of Britain's farmers to the war effort was hugely important – by the last year of the war, they provided enough food to keep Britons adequately fed for six out of seven days of the week – by itself it was not enough to enable the government to avoid bringing in food rationing.

As early as New Year 1940, Sir John Boyd Orr, well-known for his influential book, *Food, Health and Income*, published in 1936, was telling the nation, by way of the BBC's Home Service, that 'porridge and milk are better for you than bacon and butter'. Christopher Tomlin, a young writing-paper salesman, noted in the diary he kept for Mass Observation that Sir John had also said that 'potatoes are good [and that] we should grow some vegetables even if it's only in a flower pot'. Christopher thought that Sir John was making a propaganda point about the importance of avoiding imported foods, and 'growing as much as we can' because the government was scared, thinking 'we won't able to get enough food across with all those boats sunk.'

The government was indeed deeply concerned about how badly the Battle of the Atlantic was going at this time, but some sections of officialdom were also scared of the consequences of introducing food

RICE OR POTATO BREAD

375 ml scalded milk
4 teaspoons baking powder
180 g corn meal
1 teaspoon salt
1 tablespoon shortening
150 g boiled rice or fresh mashed
  potatoes
1 egg

Pour the scalded milk over corn meal and add shortening. Beat egg until very light and add slowly. Cool and add baking powder and salt. Mix well and add the rice or potatoes. Bake in greased shallow pan in hot oven for 30 minutes.

rationing. They thought that large sections of the population would be irritated and even alienated by any attempt to rein-in their choice of foods and the amounts they could buy. While such officials may have seen Sir John's promotion of potatoes, porridge and milk over bacon and butter as simply a softening-up process for the day – now imminent - when bacon, butter, eggs and much else would have to be rationed, Sir John was actually coming from a different direction altogether.

He had long seen that income was a major factor in deciding how people fed themselves. Far too many of the nation's children – between a fifth and a quarter, he calculated – came from families whose incomes were so low that their children could only be fed a diet that was seriously deficient in essential nutrients. While the government was still hesitating about introducing rationing – even though the ration books were all printed and ready to be distributed – Sir John tried to concentrate minds by pointing out that for thousands of people, 'foodstuffs have in fact always been rationed by price'.

Food rationing in Britain was announced on 8 January 1940. The government emphasised the point that rationing would ensure a fair distribution of all available food, while the way in which it was being rationed – through local shopkeepers and to people registered with their local shopkeepers – meant that prices could be controlled and would be fair.

The first foods to be rationed were bacon, ham, sugar and butter. Two months later meat, except sausages and offal, was rationed, and in July tea, margarine, cooking fat and cheese. By July 1942, jam, marmalade, treacle, syrup, eggs and milk had also been rationed or put under

never easy to keep it so saving bread was a major theme throughout the war. 'The kitchen is the key to VICTORY. Eat less bread' cried the posters, with the Ministry of Food constantly pushing the potato as an ideal substitute for bread, especially in main meals.

The bread that was most readily available for much of the war was something called the National Loaf. It was rather grey and not very exciting to eat, but was made to a recipe that was said to be full of vitamins and high in nutritional value. It also acquired an unlikely reputation, which inspired the MP and diarist

WELL STOCKED
A shopkeeper in wartime England, proudly announces the availability of stock, of which only three are rationed.

EGGLESS, FATLESS WALNUT CAKE

500 g flour
150 g chopped walnuts
240 ml milk
200 g sugar
4 teaspoons baking powder
1 good pinch salt

Mix flour, sugar and chopped walnuts together. Add salt and baking powder, and then the milk. It should be slightly wetter than an ordinary cake mixture. Pour into a greased cake tin and leave to rise for 10 minutes. Bake in a slow oven until risen and brown.

controlled distribution. Vegetables and fruits and fish were never rationed – though most exotic fruits were seldom, if ever, seen during the war – and bread, not rationed during the war, had to be for a time in 1946 because the world's wheat harvests were so poor.

Although bread was not rationed, it was

Sir Henry 'Chips' Channon to ask the minister of food, Lord Woolton at dinner in April 1942, during a discussion on the 'new vitamin bread, the National Loaf', if it was really an aphrodisiac. 'His Lordship looked startled', noted Chips Channon in his diary.

Food rationing was explained as an emergency measure attempting to ensure that everyone got a fair share of the limited food supplies then available. In fact, it would be more than fourteen years before the last foods came off the ration and people could throw away (or keep as a souvenir of a very difficult time) their ration books. In those fourteen years, the thing that Sir John Boyd Orr had hoped for since the mid-1930s, actually came to pass. A healthy diet was now enjoyed by a much larger proportion of the population than throughout modern history and many more people were aware of the importance of eating a healthy diet and knew which foods – more often than not the less expensive ones – were the nutrient-packed ones. Even such simple things as rationing bacon, for instance, had an unforeseen result: it brought bacon into the weekly diet of many people for whom it had hitherto been an occasional luxury, if it was eaten at all.

During World War One, restaurant meals had come within the government's food rationing schemes, and diners had to hand over ration coupons in restaurants. In World War Two, restaurants were kept 'off-ration'. The government explained that this was because it would be very difficult to extend the quite complicated ration coupon system to restaurants. What the government did not say was that it would actually prefer people to eat out of their homes as much as possible, partly

BREAD PUDDING

This recipe only uses a small amount of sugar which of course was rationed during World War Two. It also uses reconstituted dried egg powder, but you can use fresh eggs as these are readily available today.

225 g stale bread
50 g grated suet
25 g sugar
1 tablespoon marmalade
50 g dried fruit
1 reconstituted dried egg (or 1 fresh egg)
Milk to mix
1 teaspoon ground cinnamon

- Preheat the oven to Gas mark 4 / 180°C / 350°F.
- Put the bread into a basin and add enough cold water to cover. Leave to stand for 15 minutes and then squeeze dry with your fingers.
- Crumble the soaked bread into a basin and add all the other ingredients.
- Add enough milk to make a sticky consistency.
- Spoon into a greased tin (approx 20 cm or 8 in) and bake in the centre of the oven for an hour. Alternatively you can steam in a greased basin for two hours.
- Serve either warm or cold.

THE 'BASAL' DIET:
A Diet Too Far

In the summer of 1940, after the disaster of Dunkirk, the War Cabinet commissioned a report from the Scientific Food Committee on the foods necessary for an adequate survival diet in wartime. Here is the essential daily diet the scientists came up with:

12oz (375g) bread
1lb (500g) potatoes
2oz (60g) oatmeal
1oz (30g) fat
6oz (180g) vegetables
six-tenths of a pint (12fl oz/350ml) milk

These essentials could be supplemented either by more of the listed foods or by small quantities of cheese, pulses, meat, fish, eggs, sugar and dried fruits.

The diet was tested on a group of volunteers, none of whom reported any ill effects. The War Cabinet, from Prime Minister Churchill down, was appalled at the effect that such a diet would have on the morale of the nation and the Ministry of Food was none too happy, either.

In the diet's favour it should be said that Winston Churchill's own idea of what was an adequate diet was large; he thought the meat ration, when shown to him, was 'adequate' until it was explained that what was put in front of him was the adult ration, not for one meal but for one week. The Basal Diet was quietly shelved.

Winston Churchill, May 1940.

because it would save a family's rations and partly because restaurants and other forms of communal feeding were less likely to waste food than households.

To ensure that everyone was dealt with fairly, and to prevent any suggestion that the well-off were getting more food than everyone else because they could afford to eat out more often while still getting the same ration books and coupons, the government subjected restaurants to some quite stringent regulations. Only three courses could be served, with only one of them a 'main' course, no matter how grand the restaurant, food was simpler and a maximum price of five shillings (twenty-five pence) was set.

The 'V' in 'Victory V' meals, served in many restaurants, did not stand for 'vegetarian', but for the idea that Britain could achieve victory through food. Such meals, carefully planned to be both appetising and nutritious, were based very much on home-grown produce, showing that restaurants were doing their bit to save on shipping.

The most popular of Britain's wartime restaurants were British Restaurants, a name suggested by the prime minister. They began during the Blitz as emergency feeding centres set up in heavily bombed areas to provide good, hot meals for people who had been bombed-out. The Ministry of Food promoted the expansion of British Restaurants to a much wider population, because they could do much to improve people's nutritional intake. The emphasis was put on well-balanced, healthy meals that were remarkably cheap – about tenpence (4p) or a shilling (5p) a head.

Many British Restaurants were set up in disused buildings, such as evacuated schools

OLD MOTHER HUBBARD
The inside of a typical wartime food cupboard, providing just the essentials.

– though a former henhouse made a good home for a British Restaurant in Nottingham – and later in the war the government supplied prefabs (prefabricated buildings) that could be quickly erected on any vacant site. To save on staff, many operated a self-service system that other caterers soon adopted.

Frank Edwards, a war factory buyer from Birmingham, was very impressed by his first visit to a British Restaurant in 1943, expressing surprise in the diary he kept for

GROW FOOD
IN YOUR GARDEN
OR GET AN ALLOTMENT

GARDEN TIPS

- Grow potatoes in a barrel – this is an easy way to grow potatoes where space is limited.
- Keep weeds at bay and get fit at the same time by doing energetic hoeing.
- Start a wormery as they are not only beneficial to your soil but they will eat up your kitchen waste as well.
- Slugs are nocturnal so attacks on the beasts are highly effective after dark, especially after rain.
- Learn about companion planting to keep pests at bay.

Mass Observation at the quality of the service, the courteousness of the helpers and the most efficient manner in which it was run. Even more astonishing was actually being asked if he was hungry – 'not previously during the war have I been asked that question in a restaurant,' he wrote, while having the question followed up by 'an exceedingly generous helping' was egg on the pudding indeed. No wonder, according to two surveys carried out by the British Institute of Public Opinion in 1942 and 1944, that nearly 70 per cent of the people interviewed said they would like to see British Restaurants continuing after the war.

The government took its efforts to increase communal feeding into two other important areas, factories and schools, quite early in the war. An order issued in November 1940 made it compulsory for factories with more than 250 workers doing some form of war work to set up canteens. Workers in heavy industries, such as mining, ship-building and steel-making, got extra rations in their canteens, some of which, such as cheese, were provided through the United States' Lend-Lease programme.

Factory canteens were soon seen as ideal places in which to raise morale as well as feed workers, since happy workers were also likely to be efficient workers, willing to spend long hours at work for not very high wages. A particularly successful way of raising morale among war industry workers was to send concert parties into factory canteens during meal breaks.

The writer J.B. Priestley made good use of one of his enormously popular *Postscripts*, which was broadcast after the regular nine o'clock evening news bulletins on the BBC's

GROW YOUR OWN

Waitresses from the Quality Inn in Regent Street, London, watering and gathering tomatoes that are growing in boxes on the pavement outside the restaurant as part of the 'Dig For Victory' scheme.

Home Service. In it he described a lunch-hour ENSA (Entertainments National Service Association) performance by 'an orchestra consisting of four young women in green silk', after which the two thousand-strong audience, 'who were mostly young and feminine, and very natty in their coloured overalls, returned – much heartened – to another five or six hours'

A SATISFYING MEAL
FOR PENNIES

British Restaurants began as emergency feeding centres, provided by an organisation called Londoners' Meal Services, during the Blitz. Both organisations provided nutritious foods for amazingly low prices.

For example, the chalk board hung on the side of a Londoners' Meal Service mobile van (*below*) in 1940 offered:

Cold Roast Veal, with carrots & potatoes for 10d (4p) a plateful (with customers bringing their own plates, or maybe a neighbour's, if their own had been reduced to broken bits).

Spam sandwiches for 3d (less than 1½p)
A cup of tea for 2d (tuppence).

British Restaurants developed much more extensive menus, such as:

Lentil soup, 1d;
Rabbit pie with vegetables, 6d and 8d;
Braised liver and vegetables, 6d and 8d;
Steak and kidney pie and vegetables, 6d and 8d;
Sultana roll and rice pudding, both 2d.
Children's meals were 4d (less than 5p) each.

British Restaurants were funded by the government, through local councils, and went a long way to ensuring that, despite stringent rationing, the British people got good amounts of healthy food on a regular basis during the war. Restaurants such as the country-wide chain of Lyons' tea shops and Corner Houses provided affordable meals throughout the Blitz. It only closed for three days in September 1940 when they had no water supply. Their menu included two starters, seven main courses and a choice of four puddings.

SERVICE AS NORMAL
July 1939: The waitress is polite and courteous at the Lyon's Tea Room in Ludgate Circus as the man enjoys his last 'civvy' lunch before joining the forces.

work at their machines.'

Priestly saw 'this genial conspiracy between the Ministry of Labour and ENSA' to provide entertainment during the meal hours in both the day and the night shifts for workers in war production factories as 'a roaring success'. It was certainly great for morale.

School meals were another major way in which the authorities ensured that the population was eating well. Full meals were provided at lunchtime in schools, which also received extra free milk. As the war went on, many school canteens were able to serve the vegetables grown by pupils in their school's own vegetable plot. Even traditional nursery rhymes were adapted to encourage children to dig for victory:

There was an old woman who lived in a shoe.
She had so many children she didn't know
    what to do.
She gave them potatoes instead of some bread,
And the children were happy and very well fed.

'Eating out', at restaurants, British restaurants, factory canteens and other forms of communal eating increased enormously during the war. Strangers would share tables to save space, so that it turned it into a social occasion and an opportunity to share war stories. In an effort to get people to eat properly balanced meals during the war, many small cafés and restaurants opened providing meals such as cottage pie, steak and kidney pie, faggots and mushy peas, sausage and mash or toad in the hole. By the end of 1944, around 170,000,000 meals a week were being eaten by civilians outside the home – all of them using rationed foods, such as meat, sugar and fats, that came outside the diners' normal rations.

SCHOOL DINNERS

In 1940, the minister for food, Lord Woolton, wanted to make sure that every British child had at least one hot meal a day, so he introduced free school meals to children of poorer families. This gesture turned out to be a mixed blessing for some children, as they found themselves singled out and were made to feel different from those who didn't qualify. With the addition of free milk, cod-liver oil and orange juice to their diet, children grew generally taller and heavier than before the war so Lord Woolton's efforts were not in vain.

School dinners were usually cooked away from the school premises and then delivered in insulated metal containers. The food was nutritionally balanced so that it provided a midday meal in school to all children, giving them 40 per cent of their daily protein and 33 per cent of their daily energy needs. The government covered 70 per cent of the cost, rising in 1941 to 95 per cent. Families who were not entitled to free meals paid 5d (2p) per day.

Those schools that had their own kitchens were a far-cry from today's purpose built canteens. With their cold stone floors and basic – but functional – equipment, the dinner ladies had to do their best to turn out hundreds of nutritional meals each week.

SCHOOL DINNERS

January 1942: Schoolboys and a WVS driver unload school dinners in insulated containers at Epsom Central School.

DIGGING FOR VICTORY

One of the most important and most successful advertising and propaganda campaigns ever conducted in Britain was the one that was launched by the Ministry of Agriculture as the 'Grow More Food Campaign' in August 1939.

By itself, the campaign's title would probably have been enough to achieve its aim of getting everyone to grow more food, but the real spur to the extraordinary expansion of domestic food production during the war was the campaign's subtitle – Dig for Victory. 'Let Dig for Victory be the motto of everyone with a garden,' said the then Minister of Agriculture, Sir Reginald Dorman-Smith, a former President of the National Farmers' Union, at the outbreak of war. And every gardener – indeed, every man, woman and child able to lift a spade, a hoe and a garden fork – did just that.

Britain, of necessity, became a 'grow-your-own' country during World War Two. It was able to do so remarkably quickly and extraordinarily comprehensively because of its strong amateur gardening tradition, a tradition which by the end of the nineteenth century had extended to the thousands of small gardens in front of and behind suburban houses.

Poets wrote whole poems extolling the 'glories of the garden' and wrote about 'borders, beds and shrubberies and lawns and avenues'. While Rudyard Kipling's *The Glory of the Garden* concentrated on the grand gardens of stately homes, the houses of the well-to-do with gardens large enough to support a croquet lawn and a tennis court as well as a walled kitchen garden, and the delightful gardens to be found around English thatched country cottages, he knew full well that gardens were not made by people 'singing 'Oh, how beautiful' and sitting in the shade'.

One verse of his great poem could have stood as a call to arms for Britain's householders:

———◦◦◦———

There's not a pair of legs so thin, there's not a
*   head so thick,*
There's not a hand so weak and white, nor yet
*   a heart so sick,*
But it can find some needful job that's crying
*   to be done,*
For the Glory of the Garden glorifieth every
*   one.*

———◦◦◦———

Once war was declared everyone with a garden, large or small, worked overtime to fill it with as many food crops as possible. Later, householders with front and back gardens tended to grow flowers in the front garden, where they could gladden the hearts of passers-by, and keep the vegetable plot in the back garden, safe from pilferers.

Also potential valuable growing spaces were the public parks and gardens that, since early Victorian times, had been established in every town and city in the country; for town planners had early recognized the importance of giving cities 'lungs'. Workers could come out of their factories and the huddled, close-packed housing in which they lived to breathe the fresh air and enjoy the beautiful plants and green spaces to be found in what, by the 1930s, amounted to thousands of acres of public parks.

Even before the war began, the grass and lawns of public parks in cities up and down the land were being ploughed up and turned into allotments. The neatly hoed rows of early peas twining up sticks in the allotments surrounding the Albert Memorial in Kensington Gardens, London, photographed in 1942, were typical of scenes in public parks everywhere.

Another element in the British people's ability to feed themselves well in such a crisis as all-out war was the allotment which, from the first launching of the Dig for Victory campaign, was seen as the Ministry of Agriculture's main assistant in the task of getting Britain digging. This was largely because the National Allotments Society had many affiliated bodies of allotment holders in both town and country.

The 1908 Allotments Act obliged local authorities to set aside public land for renting to people with little or no garden space so that

BATEMANS

Batemans in Burwash, East Sussex, was the one time home of Rudyard Kipling. The house was bought in 1634 and now belongs to the National Trust.

they could grow their own food. Allotments soon came to play a big role in providing the ordinary family with fresh vegetables and fruit. During 1914–1918 the number of allotments doubled in Britain; the same thing happened during World War Two.

Greatly helped by Cultivation of Land (Allotment) Orders issued in 1939 and 1941, which allowed local authorities to take possession of any unoccupied land which could conveniently be turned into allotments, councils found extra land for allotments in public parks (Hyde Park in London, for instance) and on

OFF THE BEAT
Policemen from Peckham station in London, take a welcome break by turning over their flower beds to growing vegetables as a contribution to the 'Dig for Victory' campaign.

common land (such as Clapham Common, again in London). There were a little over 800,000 allotments in England and Wales in 1939; by 1945 the number had increased to nearly one and a half million.

During the war, all these aspects of gardening in Britain – gardens large and small, parks, both public and private, and allotments – played heroic parts in the task of keeping the nation properly fed. And they weren't the only bits of land pressed into service. Spurred on by the Ministry of Agriculture's huge Dig for

WINTER VEGETABLES

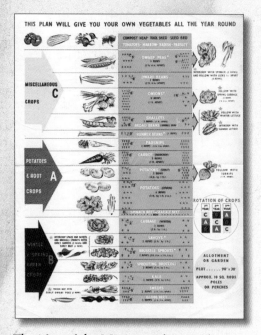

The idea of the Ministry of Agriculture's leaflets were to show people how to grow their own produce throughout the whole year. Leaflet no. 1 (*above*) explained how to prepare the ground and plan your patch for growing. Just because you have put your lawn mower away for the season, doesn't mean you have to put all your other garden tools away as well. Even without a greenhouse it is still possible to keep your kitchen garden going through the winter months. This has the bonus of giving you plenty of fresh air, much-needed exercise and delicious home-grown produce all-year round.

Produce that can be grown during the chilly winter months include:

- Broad beans
- Asparagus
- Peas, pea shoots and sugarsnap varieties
- Garlic
- Leeks
- Onions, spring onions and shallots
- Winter and lamb's lettuce
- Spinach
- Parsnips
- Spring cabbage
- Brussels sprouts

TOP TIPS

- Make sure you buy the correct variety for autumn planting so that you will always get the best from your crop.
- Don't be tempted to dig up any more than you need at any one time – the vegetables will almost always keep better in the ground. This applies particularly to potatoes, leeks and parsnips.
- Don't forget wildlife will be extra hungry during the cold winter months, so make sure you protect your crops from pests.
- Crops that have to be dug up can be hung, as in the case of onions. Shallots and onions look great plaited into an old-fashioned rope-look and will keep for months.

of land capable of supporting life, even the moat round the Tower of London, were planted with potatoes, carrots, cabbages, leeks, beetroot and much else. Garden clubs flourished during the war. Their members shared expensive and increasingly hard-to-obtain tools, offered expertise and advice to each other, and swapped seeds, seedlings and plants. Seasonal displays and shows of the produce of garden clubs and allotments associations became increasingly common as the war went on.

Ignorance of gardening and growing plants, or the frailty of the female sex were no excuse. At the head of the food-growing army stood the Ministry of Agriculture, bombarding the nation with leaflets and advertisements, organising Dig For Victory Weeks throughout the country, issuing pamphlets, posters, cropping charts, even 'Some Notes for Sermons', all exhorting everyone to dig, dig, dig for victory. The Ministry made a special target of women, because, 'while the men are away and farmers are using their fields for other vital crops, Women Must DIG'.

The Ministry provided plenty of free, well-illustrated leaflets to help them: Dig for Victory leaflet no. 20, for example, showed how to dig; leaflet no. 1 showed how to do the preliminary planning; and leaflet no. 19 explained exactly how to sow seeds. The emphasis of the newspaper and magazine ads and the leaflets was always on vegetables, especially green vegetables which children must have, and potatoes, which could replace bread. The onion was another vegetable heavily promoted by the Ministry. Until Germany invaded the Channel Islands, most of Britain's onions had come from there and this sudden cutting off of an essential vegetable hit the nation hard. Onions quickly

MAKING USE OF EVERY INCH
Not one inch of space of London was wasted during the war. After Mr Sabcha's house was bombed in Kensington, he converted the site into an allotment to grow food. Before being allowed in, visitors had to buy a Savings stamp.

Victory publicity campaign – in 1942 alone the ministry printed 10,000,000 leaflets of advice and instruction – school sports fields and playgrounds, golf courses, bomb sites, road verges, railway embankments and every scrap

NO PLACE TOO SMALL

In the inner cities, where many houses had no garden, window boxes were turned over to lettuces, herbs, carrots and even tomatoes, though the height of tomato plants meant that they cut out more of the light already reduced by the criss-cross hatching of anti-bomb taping.

The Women's Voluntary Service (WVS) was among the first to see the value of window boxes for growing not just food, but also flowers, especially in the inner cities and in bombed areas. In this the WVS was supported by the government, which encouraged the growing of flowers because their colour and scent made them good morale-boosters and also helped preserve seed stocks.

Rather larger than window boxes but also very small as growing areas were the roofs of the Anderson shelters (*above*) that

many people erected in their back yards and gardens. Much of the soil that was dug out of the garden to make space for the Anderson shelter could be put back on its corrugated iron roof to make a handily accessible place for growing beans, cabbages, marrows and other plants with shallow roots. As an American journalist commented in the summer of·1941, passers-by were in 'greater danger of being hit by a vegetable marrow falling off the roof of an air-raid shelter than of being struck by a bomb'.

As with window boxes, so Anderson shelters were also used for growing flowers. As early as autumn 1939, one gardening catalogue was offering collections of plants such as berberis, cotoneaster and cydonia that would make good covering mounds for air-raid shelters.

THE VICTORY GARDEN

PLANT A VICTORY GARDEN

OUR FOOD IS FIGHTING

A GARDEN WILL MAKE YOUR RATIONS GO FURTHER

Victory Gardens, also known as war gardens or food gardens for defence, were designed to grow vegetables, fruits and herbs. Because labour and transportation difficulties during the war made it hard to harvest and move vegetables and fruit to market, the government turned to the people of Britain to plant Victory Gardens. The aim was to get citizens to provide their own fresh produce so that no one went without. Anyone who had any spare space – whether it was on their large country estate, in an empty lot where houses had been destroyed, public parks and even on rooftops – was encouraged to plant produce all in the name of patriotism. Portions of Hyde Park in London and San Francisco's Golden Gate Park were ploughed for plots to give city dwellers access to land for growing produce.

Magazines gave instructions on what and how to plant and ways of preserving the produce. The idea quickly caught on and it rapidly became a massive community effort. It was a way for individuals to feel they were doing their part on the home front and the campaign was a tremendous success.

When World War Two ended, so did the government's promotion of victory gardens. In their elation at the news that the war had ended, people failed to grow fruit and vegetables in the spring of 1946. Unfortunately the farmers had not geared up their production to cope with the demand and the country experienced certain food shortages.

Victory gardens were not just the idea of the United Kingdom, citizens in the United States, Canada, Germany and Australia also did their part.

became a luxury food, so valuable that they could make welcome items in charity auctions.

All you had to do to get the Ministry's leaflets, which were promoted in hundreds of newspaper and magazine advertisements, was to fill in the coupon at the foot of the ad, put it in an unsealed envelope (cheap to post because it only needed a one penny stamp) and send it off to the Ministry, whose leaflet department was safely out of the bomber's way in the Hotel Lindum in St Anne's-on-Sea, Lancs.

Almost as helpful to the amateur gardener was the BBC's Home Service, whose managers were cajoled, even bullied, into service as providers of gardening information by the men of the Ministry of Agriculture's wartime Advisory Committee on Publicity. The Brains Trust regularly featured agricultural experts and there was a special 'Radio Allotment' programme. For this programme one of its presenters, the well-known Mr Middleton, kept his own allotment. His very helpful advice was underpinned by constant morale boosting and such exhortations as 'save our seeds' and 'turn our gardens into munition factories, for potatoes, carrots and onions are munitions of war as much as shells and bullets are'.

The Ministry of Agriculture's booklet, *Spring Wartime Gardening Guide*, issued in support of the 'Dig for Victory' Campaign, was given extra sales potential by being edited by Roy Hay, a well-known presenter on 'Radio Allotment' (and also a member of the Ministry's advisory publicity committee). Roy Hay's familiarity to gardeners stood him in good stead after the war, for his gardening books were strong sellers for several decades.

One of agriculture's main problems during the war was filling the gap in livestock

TOMATOES IN THE WINDOW
Window boxes in this urban block of flats are being used to raise tomatoes to supplement wartime shortages.

production caused by the heavy drop in the import of feeding stuffs: from 8,500,000 tons a year to 1,125,000 tons after four years of war. Before the war, many small farms grew very little animal feed-stuffs, relying on imports, with some grazing and water, to do all that was necessary for their animals to produce milk, eggs and meat, especially pork. Turning

SUBURBAN SWAP SHOPS

Once digging for victory was well under way in suburban gardens and allotments, bartering their products began to be another aspect of the national effort to pull together for victory. It has been estimated that bartering was going on in earnest from the summer of 1941, and was a perfectly acceptable habit. It had nothing to do with the blackmarket in food, especially meat, which went on during the war. Rather, bartering was all about one neighbour helping another.

Few gardeners could grow every type of vegetable they would need in the kitchen, so they might swap some of their glut of spring onions, for instance, for one or two cabbages from next door, or green beans for carrots… Or perhaps your allotment soil was proving all wrong for spring onions, but could manage something that your neighbour did not grow. Vegetables could also be swapped for other services: give some tomatoes and potatoes to the old lady next door who does not have a garden and she will do that difficult job of turning the collar of your husband's best shirt, perhaps, or darn a few socks for you.

Often, local greengrocers, having difficulties getting regular deliveries, would buy up back garden and allotment

surpluses, and sell them on to their many customers who had no access to home-grown vegetables. Local shopkeepers also made use of the regular 'barter markets' established in many local communities. Here, there would be a much wider range of vegetables and other foods available for swapping.

many acres of their farms over to animal food, as well as to the wheat and potatoes that the government was ordering them to grow for human consumption, meant that there was less room for livestock.

Poultry numbers on large farms were considerably reduced, so that farm egg production quickly fell to half what it had been before the war, and farm pig numbers were also cut. The amateur gardener and the householder stepped into the breach, with great numbers of them taking enthusiastically to keeping livestock, especially hens and pigs, but also rabbits and ducks and even goats.

During the war, the main producers of pig meat, especially bacon, but also pork, and hens' eggs became small general farmers, cottage gardeners and the owners of suburban back gardens. All these people were buoyed up by the knowledge, continually drummed into them by officialdom, that the imported grain the pigs were used to feeding on would

WARTIME CITY PIGS
April 1943: A National fire officer rounds up a group of pigs on the bomb site of the Museum of the Royal College of Surgeons in Central London. He and his colleagues have shares in a pig rearing club which they operate on the site.

have to be substituted. This was so that space could be freed up on trans-Atlantic shipping for aeroplanes and armaments that the United States was sending to Britain. In short, by changing the pigs' diet the farmer could help equip Britain's army.

With such facts to spur them on, it is perhaps not surprising that domestic poultry keepers, who were keeping some 6,470,000 fowls in 1939, had increased their flocks to 10,772,000 by 1944–45. Over the same years, egg output increased from 650 million to 970 million. As for pigs reared on holdings of less than an acre, the figures for numbers slaughtered went up from 272 million in 1939 to 323 million in 1944–45. And most of this was achieved on a hen and pig diet based very largely on kitchen scraps.

Hens were relatively easy to keep in the garden and could be kept well fed with kitchen scraps. Many a home kept a galvanised bucket

WARTIME CHICKS

September 1939: A young evacuee makes friends with tiny new-born chicks on a farm in Hertfordshire. With her is a land girl who has the task of ensuring food production during wartime.

HAPPY WELL-FED PIGS AND HENS

Despite the sudden disappearance of their pre-war diet of largely imported grain (mostly barley) and maize meal mash, the British pig did not do badly during the war. As the Minister of Agriculture pointed out reassuringly at the start of the war, the pig is an omnivorous animal and 'will thrive on food usually wasted, such as chat potatoes, house scraps and garden refuse for the fattening pig, and acorns and beechmast for the breeding pig'.

Pigswill bins, for collecting kitchen waste and food scraps, were put out on the streets by councils up and down the country. The bins were collected regularly and their contents processed into a nutritious feed that both pigs and hens could feed well on.

The version of concentrated kitchen waste produced in the city of Bristol from RAF, army and factory canteen kitchens as well as from domestic kitchens, came to be called 'Bristol Pudding' – a not surprising name, given that it was dark brown in colour and had the texture and consistency of prune mould. In hot weather it quickly began to give off an appalling smell. The hens on Rainscombe Farm in Wiltshire, owned by Anthony Hurd, one of the Minister of Agriculture's liaison officers, didn't mind. 'They eagerly picked over this mess and found some sustenance,' Mr Hurd recalled in his book *A Farmer in Whitehall*. 'Teaspoons, metal tops of milk bottles, and false teeth they discarded.' Clearly, not all Bristol householders heeded the standard advice for kitchen waste put into council street pig food bins: 'Keep it dry, free from glass, bones, metal, paper, etc.'

PIG FOOD COLLECTOR
August 1940: A worker from the WVS supervises a woman as she empties household waste into a separate rubbish bin for pig feed. This was a novel scheme in the London borough of Westminster.

SOLDIERS PLAY THEIR PART

January 1941: Even soldiers were not exempt from playing their part in supplying Britain with food. These men are from the Infantry Training Centre in Eastern Command where they kept over seventy pigs.

in the kitchen into which went such things as potato peelings, cabbage stalks, vegetable trimmings and stale bread crusts. These were boiled up every day, and although the result might smell horrid, the hens thrived on it.

By 1943–4, domestic and small farm poultry keepers were producing about a quarter of the country's officially known supplies of eggs, despite the fact that many henhouses in back gardens provided eggs just for the housewife,

her family and her friends, with perhaps a few going to the local grocer with whom she was registered (a few eggs 'under the counter' might get her something else on top of her ration allowance). At war's end, the Domestic Poultry Keepers' Council (by this time also responsible for domestic rabbit production) had one and a quarter million members, keeping some twelve million hens.

Despite these valiant efforts, domestic

USEFUL TIPS ON KEEPING PIGS

KEEP A PIG

SAVE Waste and make FOOD

FOR ADVICE AND INFORMATION ABOUT PIG CLUBS APPLY TO –
SMALL PIG KEEPERS' COUNCIL, VICTORIA HOUSE, SOUTHAMPTON ROW, W.C.1.

THRIFTY TIP

- Make enclosures pig proof as they are great escape artists.
- Pigs love attention and love a scratch behind the ear or a rub down with a brush. However, never slap a pig on its backside as they hate this and can sulk for days.
- Pigs are voracious eaters and will eat virtually anything – including a stray finger if you leave it too long in the trough!

- Their smelling abilities make them perfect pets for sniffing out truffles.
- If you make cheese, they love eating the excess whey milk.
- Pink-skinned pigs can suffer from sunburn so make sure they have adequate shelter.
- Always try to choose a pig with a gentle temperament otherwise it could show aggression to you, your children and other pigs.
- Make sure fresh, clean water is available at all times of the day and night.
- Make sure your troughs are tough and heavy as pigs have a habit of moving them about.
- Feed your pigs on household scraps or old crops from your vegetable garden. Remember though, pigs will not eat citrus fruit, peppers, onions, pineapples and certain brassicas.
- Your pig will love a bed of deep clean straw of litter. Pigs will not soil their bedding, they would rather choose a corner of their pen.
- Pigs are wallowers and love nothing more than rolling around in a mud bath.
- Each pig should have at least 8 sq feet of space and the floor should be concrete so that your pig has sure footing at all times.
- Pigs do not like cold winds or draughts, so make sure your pig sty is insulated.

poultry keepers and large-scale poultry farmers were not able to keep the country supplied with enough shell eggs to allow everyone to enjoy their pre-war average of three eggs a week. By mid-war most people were seeing just one shell egg a fortnight, and often none for long periods. In 1941, the first dried eggs, mostly from America, via the Lend-Lease programme, reached Britain.

Pig-keeping became very popular with people with enough land, such as an allotment or a reasonably-sized back garden with room for a pig; and with groups of people, especially men working together in places like air raid wardens' posts and fire stations, but also the regulars of public houses. The Ministry of Food called such people 'small pig keepers'. They were permitted to keep and kill a pig provided that it was to be consumed by them and their families, that they had had it for fattening for at least two months and that they obtained a licence to slaughter from their local Food Control Committee. One of the smaller heartaches of the war was the very real distress caused when the inevitable last day in the back garden came for the family pig – especially if it had become such a friend that it followed the children to school.

In November 1939, the Small Pig Keepers' Council was formed to encourage allotment holders, cottagers and suburban householders to keep pigs, and to assist in the formation of pig clubs. Pig Clubs were formed in large numbers: there was even one in the London Zoo, set up by thirty staff members, including several keepers, who fed their pigs from the zoo restaurant's kitchen waste (with the kitchen eventually getting its waste back in the form of bacon). By mid-war there were nearly seven thousand Pig Clubs in Britain, with hundreds of thousands of members.

The great value of Pig Clubs to the small pig keeper lay in the fund of knowledge about pig-keeping they possessed and, more practically, the fact that members could obtain their licence for slaughtering – granted for the slaughter of one pig in three months or two pigs in six months – through the Pig Club. Members of Pig Clubs could also sell their fattened pigs to a local retail butcher (at a price not exceeding 'the wholesale price for the time being', said the price-control-conscious Ministry of Food).

Although it was not possible to give totally accurate figures for the amount of food grown by Diggers for Victory during the war, it was estimated shortly afterwards that in England and Wales some 2,500,000 to 3,000,000 tons of food came from allotments and gardens: a quite remarkable tribute to ordinary men and women doing their best in very troubled times.

PIGS AT LONDON ZOO
September 1940: Zoo keepers at London Zoo with three piggy friends.

THRIFTY TIP
THE UNITED KINGDOM
THE UNITED KINGDOM

THE PERFECT SITE FOR GROWING FRUIT AND VEG

Follow these simple instructions on how to prepare your soil and you should very quickly reap the rewards by eating fresher and tastier vegetables than you can buy in any supermarket. Just like the poster says – Dig for Victory.

- Firstly make sure your plot has access to plenty of sunshine as most vegetables will need at least six to eight hours of sunlight a day.

- Make sure the site is in close proximity to a water supply.
- Protect your site with a fence to keep out rabbits and any other animals that may damage your crops.
- Dig over the entire site to a depth of around 8–10 inches and continue to work the soil until it is loose and friable (easily crumbled).
- Improve the condition of the soil by adding some organic matter as this releases nitrogen, minerals and other nutrients for plants as it decays. Well rotted compost or manure is ideal for this purpose.
- Before you start planting consider the layout of your beds. Make sure you have enough space between the rows.
- Practice crop rotation as growing the same vegetables year after year in the same bed can lead to an increased risk of disease.
- Find out which companion plants go with which vegetable to minimise the risk of damage by pests.
- Hoe your beds regularly to keep on top of the weeds and leave the soil in a loose, friable condition to absorb maximum rainfall.
- Make sure you water regularly, your vegetables will require a minimum of one inch of water each week. Water early in the morning to avoid evaporation by the sun.

IN THE KITCHEN

The kitchen that was the province of the average wartime housewife was a very different affair from the one her grandmother had known. Not that most housewives could now be called 'average', since they probably also either had a full-time job or spent many hours of every week making a great contribution to the war effort by working with voluntary organisations like the Red Cross, the Women's Voluntary Service (WVS) and the Women's Institute (WI).

It was during the war that the concept of the married woman as a sort of housewife superwoman, able to hold down a full-time job and be a full-time housekeeper, wife and mother as well, became reality. As the war dragged on, more and more women were drawn into industry, agriculture and the armed forces, or into Civil Defence, so that by 1944, seven million of the sixteen million women in Britain aged between fourteen and fifty-nine were employed in these areas. Several million more worked outside the home for many hours every week doing essential voluntary work or replacing men on active service in jobs in public transport and similar areas.

The average kitchen in 1939 was quite small – small enough for many women to call it their 'kitchenette' – and was designed with the convenience of one person, the housewife, rather than a cook and other domestic staff, in mind. Many women who began the war with a cook in the kitchen, lost her during the war, usually to some form of war service, but also

for family reasons. Virginia Woolf's Mabel, who had been the cook in the Woolf household for five years, left in 1940, as the Battle of Britain was at its height, to live with her sister.

For many upper-middle-class women, keeping their domestic staff was a matter of honour. One day in May 1940, Virginia Woolf drove past a friend's garden and saw her 'in an old garden hat weeding. Out comes a maid in muslin apron and cap tied with blue riband. 'Why?', wondered Mrs Woolf in her diary. 'To keep up standards of civilisation?'. Well, yes, but the war was only just coming to the end of its 'phoney' stage on the Home Front, and soldiers snatched from the beaches of Dunkirk were only just beginning to get back home. Such 'civilised standards' as maids in caps and muslin aprons would soon disappear from domestic life.

Many ordinary housewives also lost their daily helps, as both girls and married women quickly discovered they could earn much more in the local war industry factory than by doing

HOW TO TRUSS A CHICKEN

You might think that trussing a chicken is a difficult procedure – not at all. Trussing is a simple procedure that enhances a chicken's flavour and presentation. If you have stuffed the inside of the bird, trussing makes sure that it doesn't fall out.

- The first job is to clean the chicken inside and out and dry thoroughly using kitchen paper.
- Now take a reasonable length of kitchen string and put it under the base of the chicken's neck and then around the wings and legs.
- Cross the string under the legs, cross both legs and then loop the string around them first from the right side and then from the left side, twice.
- Tighten the string, then bring it back to the top. Make a double knot, then make a second double knot before trimming off the string.
- Your chicken is now ready to be cooked.

THRIFTY TIP

A HELPING HAND
Many women who began the war with a cook in their kitchen, lost her to some form of war service.

the cleaning in another woman's house. Nella Last, desperate for help to keep her little house in Barrow-in-Furness neat and clean, could afford to have help just one day a week because the going rate – 3s 6d (about 32p) a day – was as much as she could afford by the end of 1941 – far below what the hourly rate in a war industry factory added up to for a day's work.

The coal-fired kitchen range had already gone, replaced by a compact gas cooker. Lighting was either gas or electricity, with the latter available, at the immensely convenient

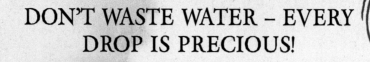

DON'T WASTE WATER – EVERY DROP IS PRECIOUS!

- Don't throw away your washing up water, save it and water your plants.
- If you wash dishes by hand, make sure you do it right after you use them, that way the food doesn't stick to them and you can use less water.
- Make the most of your washing machine by always running full loads.
- Select the short cycle option on both your dishwasher and washing machine.

'flick of a switch', in about 70 per cent of homes by 1939. Hot and cold water came out of taps set over a kitchen sink that was often placed under a window so that the housewife had a view as she worked. There were few refrigerators, so keeping food fresh and wholesome for weeks at a time was not easy, especially in the summer.

This was the typical kitchen in the houses of villages, towns and cities, but not yet in the majority of farms. A national farm survey conducted mid-way through the war found that electricity, mostly from the public supply but in one out of ten cases from private plants, had found its way into 78,000 farms in England and Wales, which was 47 per cent of the total number of occupied and working farms. The main item that the farmhouse kitchen shared with other wartime kitchens was a good, solid kitchen table that everyone could slide under when enemy bombers were heard overhead.

The relatively simple matter of buying food and getting it into the kitchen became a major undertaking during the war. Wartime food rationing, with its ration books and coupons, was based on a system that put an extra burden on the housewife, forcing her to shop regularly, at specific shops, with which she had registered, for specific foods.

Most days of the week she would have to stand in queues to obtain her rations and to buy other food and household supplies, including rationed goods like soap, in amounts that she could carry home herself, for most delivery vans and boys on a bike soon disappeared. It was a good idea to get down to the shops early, while stocks were high, waiting only to listen to the *Food Front* programme after the 8 a.m. BBC Home Service news broadcast to discover what was currently available and to get some ideas for preparing and cooking it.

BREAD STUFFING

This recipe is a way of using up bread that is not fresh enough to use for sandwiches. It can either be placed inside the carcass of your chicken or turkey, or made into stuffing balls as an accompaniment to your Sunday roast.

1 loaf of bread
1– 2 oz butter
1 garlic clove
1 onion
Fresh herbs such as sage, thyme and parsley
500 ml of vegetable or chicken stock

- Tear your bread into small pieces and place in a large bowl. Chop the herbs and season with salt and pepper.
- Dot the butter over the top.
- Chop the onion and garlic finely and saute in butter. Add to the bowl of bread and mix thoroughly.
- Take the warm stock and pour a little over the bread until it is moist but not too wet. Stir until it starts to stick together.
- Either stuff your chicken or roll into balls using your hands.
- Cook in the oven at about 200°C / 390°F / Gas 6 for about 30 to 40 minutes or until golden brown, turning once during cooking.

THE LUXURY OF RUNNING WATER
Many homes had the luxury of hot and cold running water at the kitchen sink.

As the war went on, ways had to be found to help women in full-time work actually to get their rationed foods – and, indeed, any shopping at all. Mass Observation made a detailed survey of people working in wartime production called *People in Production*. It was published first in hardback and then, presumably because of the public interest in the subject, as a paperback Penguin Special in 1942.

FARMHOUSE GINGER BEER

When schoolgirl Georgina Plumb was evacuated with the other girls in her school from Bromley, on the outskirts of London in September 1939, she fetched up in a large farmhouse in the Kent countryside. The farm had no electricity and no running water. All water had to be brought in from a pond in one of the farm's fields and boiled before being used for cooking and drinking. Ginger was added to the boiled pond water, which tasted nasty, to make it palatable.

There were plenty of compensations, as Georgina, now Gina Hughes, recalled years later in her book *Harvest of Memories*. To begin with, there was bacon from the farm's pigs and two eggs from its hens, for breakfast every morning. Later, although she hated seeing rabbits shot, she discovered the 'wonderful' taste of a casserole made from those rabbits, cooked with onions and freshly chopped sage, both of them grown on the farm. The rabbits' skins were not wasted. Like mole skins, they were stretched out on boards and treated to a drying process that enabled them to be sold.

Here is an old wartime recipe for Ginger Wine and it is well worth the effort.

1 gallon (4.5 litres) cold water
3¼ lb (1.5 kg) sugar
1.5 oz (45 g) bruised ginger
1 oz (30 g) split seeded raisins
2 lemons
2 juicy oranges (Seville are the best)
1 sweet orange
½ oz (15 g) compressed yeast

• Remove the the skin from the oranges and lemons without taking the white pith as this will make the wine bitter. Put the skins in with the sugar, ginger, raisins and water and then add the juice from the fruit.
• Leave for three days stirring at intervals.
• Strain and add the yeast to the liquid and pour into a cask or demijohn and leave for one week.
• Bottle and cork and leave to mature for at least three months.

WARTIME RECIPE
THE UNITED KINGDOM

The Mass Observation interviewers quickly discovered that all the difficulties involved in getting time off work, in getting the shopping done in the time available, and of losing pay if they were late back to their machines, added to all the 'present war-time difficulties', were putting a considerable burden on women workers – the 'main new reservoir for production in 1942'. If something wasn't done about it, the result could be poor time-keeping and a considerable loss of morale among women workers.

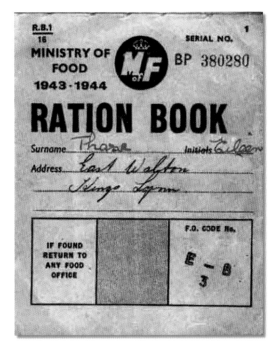

THE POINTS SYSTEM
A shopper examines the point system chart register for the new ration books.

While some major war industry companies refused to allow their workers any extra shopping time, many did help, mostly by giving workers extra time off for shopping, agreed by arrangement with section foremen. Some factories set up allotments in their grounds and sold off the produce at wholesale prices to their workers. In some places, the WVS ran shopping services, providing books in which women wrote their requirements and put the money to pay for them in an attached bag. The WVS representative took the book and money away in the morning, and returned the book and goods in the evening.

Just as Diggers for Victory got plenty of help and advice from the Ministry of Agriculture, so the Ministry of Food, headed by the very popular Lord Woolton, appointed Minister of Food in 1940 (and remaining in the job until he was made Minister for Reconstruction in November 1943), provided a very full advice service for the women in Britain's kitchens – the troops on the Kitchen Front. From the first days of the war, the Ministry of Food delivered its message in fighting terms:

WOOLTON PIE

LORD WOOLTON PIE

THE OFFICIAL RECIPE

In hotels and restaurants, no less than in communal canteens, many people have tasted Lord Woolton pie and pronounced it good. Like many another economical dish, it can be described as wholesome fare. It also meets the dietician's requirements in certain vitamins. The ingredients can be varied according to the vegetables in season. Here is the official recipe:—

Take 1lb. each diced of potatoes, cauliflower, swedes, and carrots, three or four spring onions—if possible, one teaspoonful of vegetable extract, and one tablespoonful of oatmeal. Cook all together for 10 minutes with just enough water to cover. Stir occasionally to prevent the mixture from sticking. Allow to cool; put into a piedish, sprinkle with chopped parsley, and cover with a crust of potato or wheatmeal pastry. Bake in a moderate oven until the pastry is nicely browned and serve hot with a brown gravy.

A chef in the kitchens of the grand Savoy Hotel originally dreamt up Woolton Pie, which appeared on the Savoy's menu as 'Lord Woolton's Vegetable Pie'. One version of the recipe called for 1lb (450g) of diced vegetables, with potato, swede, cauliflower and carrot suggested as a good mixture. To these could be added 3 or 4 spring onions ('if possible', said the recipe, using two words that, along with 'if available', appeared again and again in writing about food in wartime), 1 teaspoonful of vegetable extract and 1 tablespoon of oatmeal.

This version of Woolton Pie ticked all the right essential foods boxes, even managing to include oatmeal. As the war dragged on, other, slightly more sophisticated versions of Woolton Pie were cooked, including plenty of herbs and often involving a tasty sauce, such as a cheese sauce, as a topping.

Thanks to government planning, the foods that will feed you and your family to the pitch of fighting fitness are right at your hand. They have been deliberately chosen for the purpose. To release ships and seamen on the fighting fronts, you, on the 'Kitchen Front', have the job of using these foods to the greatest advantage.

The Ministry put these 'deliberately chosen' foods into three groups:

- Everyone's rations and allowances, which were the foundation of the nation's fighting diet.
- Vegetables, which provided many vitamins, important not only for good health but also for that other wartime essential, 'buoyant vitality'.
- Unrefined or wholegrain foods, which pro-vided both valuable health factors and bulk, to help build up satisfying meals.

Throughout the war the Ministry promoted these three food groups in a publicity campaign that rivalled the Agriculture Ministry's one in scale and extent. Every time the Ministry developed a new policy, Lord Woolton would explain it himself on the wireless, usually in a broadcast lasting more than ten minutes (and into which he had put several hours of preparatory work). There were hundreds of advice, instruction and recipe leaflets putting forward 'Food Facts', which were distributed to newspapers, magazines and welfare centres. Public broadcasting was

THE ROLE OF THE CARROT IN THE WAR

Here's the man who ploughs the fields.

Here's the girl who lifts up the yield.

Here's the man who deals with the clamp, so that millions of jaws can chew and champ.

That's the story and here's the star,

Potato Pete

eat up,

ta ta!

Doctor Carrot – the children's best friend – had arrived. Carrots were the one vegetable that was in plentiful supply during World War Two and the Ministry of Agriculture promoted them heavily as a substitute for more scarce vegetables. They also advertised them as a sweetener in desserts in the absence of sugar, which was rationed to 8 oz per adult per week. Children could even enjoy an iced carrot on a stick to take the place of ice cream.

In 1941, Walt Disney even offered to promote the carrot as a nutritious food source, but as the Ministry of Food had already used their own Doctor Carrot in their promotions the characters of Carroty George, Clara Carrot and Pop Carrot were never used.

At one time there was such a glut of carrots that the Ministry let it slip that the carotene in this nutritious vegetable helped considerably with night vision and that it was responsible for the RAF's increasing success in shooting down enemy planes. Of course the population believed what they heard and the demand for carrots grew as people believed it would help them to see more clearly during the blackout hours. It was a clever ruse that worked and more and more recipes appeared in magazines to jazz up the otherwise rather bland vegetable.

As well as the Doctor Carrot character, there was also Potato Pete who was introduced for the same reason, to encourage the population to eat home grown vegetables.

The Ministry of Food introduced a bedtime story to encourage people not to waste food:

Once upon a time there were five housewives. Their names were Lady Peel-potatoes, the Hon. Mrs Waste-fuel, Miss Pour-the-vegetable-water-down-the-sink, Mrs Don't-like-uncooked-vegetables, and Mrs Won't-eat-carrots. Don't let one of them put a nose in your kitchen.

fully utilised, and regular Home Service radio programmes, particularly *Kitchen Front*, which was broadcast every weekday morning, were devoted to food and its importance for good health.

One of food and nutrition's most effective wartime radio promoters was, in fact, a man who spent much of his time on the radio talking about the healthy functioning of everyone's inner workings. Dr Charles Hill, *The Radio Doctor*, began broadcasting in 1941 a series of talks that went on for ten years. The housewives who listened to his many, lively contributions to 'Food Front' got as much valuable advice on preparing foods – 'vitamins *can't* be washed off vegetables, but they *can* be cooked out, and that's a form of wastage', he once said – as they did on the nutritional value of foods.

Dr Hill said that if he was allowed to say only three things on the 'Food Front' – and he meant the food front of the Home Front as much as he meant the radio programme – they would be to recommend everyone to 'eat some raw green vegetables every day, I would praise milk and more milk and I would preach the virtues of the food which contains so much nutriment – cheese.'

The Ministry of Food sent an army of Home Economists from its Food Advice Division up and down the country talking about food and giving advice. One of the best known of those Home Economists, Marguerite Patten, has told how she and her colleagues would set up their small portable cookers on stalls in outdoor markets, large shops (one of her 'beats' was the famous Harrods department store in London), factory canteens, village halls, hospital out-patients departments and welfare clinics. 'Our campaign was to find people, wherever they might be, and make them aware of the importance of keeping their families well fed on the rations available.'

One of the Ministry Home Economists' main advice themes was what to do, not with rationed foods, but with vegetables. These were home-grown foods, available from one's own kitchen garden or allotment as well as the nation's farms, they took up no room in ships from overseas, were not rationed, and were easy to deal with in the kitchen.

The great importance of vegetables in a healthy, nutritious diet could not be over-emphasised. It was not surprising that the most famous dish to come out World War Two, Woolton Pie – 'steak and kidney pie without the steak and kidney' – was named after the Minister of Food, since he made the promotion of vegetables, especially the potato and the carrot, a personal crusade. Both vegetables became promotional figures, called 'Potato Pete' and 'Dr Carrot', that figured largely in the Ministry of Food's propaganda campaign.

The housewife soon learned to use every part of the vegetables in her kitchen, as well as the water they were cooked in, which was carefully kept for use as stocks or in soup. The 'waste not, want not' rule extended to things like the tough, outer leaves of cabbages, which were added to soups to give flavour and bulk, and to the pods of garden peas.

The wartime housewife did not encounter such fine varieties of pea as mange-tout or sugar-snap peas, and tended to shell her peas and throw out the pods, or use them in hen feed and pigswill. 'No, no,' said the Ministry of Food, coming up with a tasty recipe for cooking pea pods, mint, a potato, onion or spring onion (if available) and salt and pepper in water until

WARTIME SOUPS

CARROT AND ONION

12 oz carrots
8 oz onions
1 pint water
¼ pint milk
salt and pepper
teaspoon yeast extract (or Marmite)
parsley to taste

- Finely chop the onions and carrots and cook them in 1 pint of water until soft, this will take about 30 minutes.
- Stir in seasoning and yeast extract and the milk and bring back up to the boil.
- Stir in the parsley and serve.

CABBAGE AND ONION

1 teaspoon butter
2 onions
2 large handfuls of finely shredded cabbage
2 vegetable stock cubes
selection of fresh herbs
salt and pepper to taste
100 g pearl barley

- Chop the onions and sauté in the butter until they are soft.
- Add warm vegetable stock and when hot add the pearl barley and stir. Simmer, covered, for 25 minutes.
- Add the shredded cabbage, herbs and season to taste. Cover again and slow simmer for a further 20 minutes.

tender. This mixture was then rubbed through a sieve and returned to the saucepan, with a flour and water thickening mixed in to make the soup creamy. It was served very hot.

Lacking as she did safe, long-term storage for fresh foods, the wartime housewife became skilled at preserving them. Bottling and jam-making, provided the Ministry of Food had made available sufficient quantities of precious sugar, were the easiest ways to deal with fruit, and with some vegetables, such as tomatoes. Nella Last was annoyed by what she saw as the 'shocking waste of sugar in confectioners' windows' ('didn't the War Cabinet, which would be the better for a few women in it, realise', she wrote in her diary, 'that it would be better to let people have sugar for jam?'). The Ministry of Food did, in fact, do its best to see that there was enough sugar available to turn the country's precious harvest of berry fruits into jam, adding an extra two pounds of sugar to the ration at harvest time.

At fruit harvest times, Ministry of Food Home Economists helped to set up Fruit Preservation Centres in those parts of the country with large fruit crops, partly to offer advice and help with using perhaps unfamiliar hedgerow berries as well as the familiar locally grown fruit, and partly to ensure that the Ministry's precious supplies of sugar were properly used. There were also many officially-recognized jam-making centres, often in someone's own kitchen, where women gathered together to make jam with local fruits and the extra jam-making sugar ration.

Marguerite Patten got used to doing polite battle with experienced housewives who had 'been making jam since before you were born, young woman' in order to persuade them that

for their jam to keep well under all conditions, it must contain 60 per cent sugar and it must be carefully and tightly sealed. There was an official recipe for weak or 'runny' jam which used the minimum sugar, but which had to be eaten within two months of its making, otherwise it would go mouldy and the precious fruit and sugar would be wasted.

Often, housewives could not get enough fruit to make more than a pot or two of jam on its own, and would eke it out by adding vegetables such as carrots (to add sweetness), swedes, turnips and marrows to the mixture. As for a perfect, Seville orange-based marmalade, well, that became just a dream for jam-makers.

When dessert oranges did make it into Britain during the war, they were given to children first, with adults getting any that were left over. Once the oranges had been eaten, however, an acceptable marmalade could be made from orange peel, with cooking apples added to the mixture. At least it was marmalade of a sort and was better than nothing – certainly better than the carrot marmalade advocated by the Ministry of Food. In October 1942, Frank Cooper, maker of the country's favourite 'Oxford' marmalade, took advertising space to tell Britain that 'owing to the requisitioning of our factory at Oxford by the Government we regret that the manufacture of Oxford Marmalade must cease until after the War'. At much the same time James Robertson and Sons had to admit that 'Total War Effort demands the withdrawal of 'Golden Shred', the world's best marmalade. It will return with VICTORY'.

Drying, pickling and salting were all used by the wartime housewife to preserve both fruits and vegetables. Drying fruit and vegetables had not been much practiced in England before

A LESSON IN PRESERVES
A member of the Women's Institute in Monmouthshire gives a talk to other members on methods of fruit and vegetable canning, bottling and drying, and jam and jelly making.

the war, since the climate was hardly suited to outdoor drying, but now that there was a war on, things were different. Housewives were advised to use a cool oven, a shelf in the airing cupboard, or the heat rising from boilers and radiators to dry such things as apples, pears, grapes, stone fruit, mushrooms and onions. The important point was that the temperature should not rise above 140°F, otherwise the

foods being dried could develop moulds.

As for salting, a common sight in wartime kitchens or larders was a crock of salted green beans. Schoolgirl Georgina Plumb recalled watching the farmer's daughter at the Kent farm to which she had been evacuated prepare runner beans for salting. 'Floss cut [them] into thicker pieces than she would normally do when cooking them straight from the garden,

MINISTRY OF FOOD LEAFLETS

The Ministry of Food issued an assortment of leaflets on how to make food tasty and still retain all the nourishment. They covered a wide variety of dishes included Cooking White Fish, Using Cheese for Breakfast, Lunch and Dinner and an assortment of War Cookery Leaflets (*left*). The Ministry also employed food advisers who were trained as home economists. Their role was to demonstrate to housewives how to make interesting and nutritional meals despite the constraints of rationing.

layering them in a big stone crock with handfuls of coarse salt. A few days later more would be added and in time the juice from the beans with the salt made a brine, which preserved the beans for months and were so useful in the winter. They were well rinsed before going into the saucepan and no further salt was added.'

Some people recalled salted beans with loathing after the war, but perhaps theirs had not been properly rinsed because Georgina felt that, although nothing could beat fresh runner beans, preserved ones were a good vegetable in bad weather when all was frozen to the ground.

Fresh eggs were another food that could be preserved quite successfully in the kitchen. They were preserved in isinglass, a form of watery gelatine obtained from fish bladders, which prevented air getting through the shells of the eggs. 'Water-glass buckets' filled

with eggs were to be found in many kitchens during the war. Even after dried eggs began coming into the country in 1941, as part of the American Lend-Lease programme, many people preferred to preserve fresh eggs – if they could get them.

Although fish was not rationed during the war, it was seldom available in any quantity, and gave the Food Ministry's Home Economists quite a lot of trouble, especially when they had to 'talk up' the wonders of unfamiliar fish like snoek (or snook), a fish from South African waters, whalemeat (not a fish, but treated as such), or fresh-salted cod, most of which came from Iceland. The price of fresh fish soared during the war. Fishermen whose boats had not been requisitioned by the navy and were able to crew them, perhaps putting a machine gun on deck to fight the Luftwaffe planes that bombed and strafed them in the North

USING DRIED-EGG POWDER

THE UNITED KINGDOM
THRIFTY
TIP
THE UNITED KINGDOM

The Ministry of Food had a hard task promoting dried-egg powder when it first became available as part of the rationing, for most people were suspicious of it. 'DRIED EGGS are my eggs – my whole eggs and nothing but my eggs' said an alert-looking hen strutting across the top of a well-known Ministry of Food leaflet.

The Ministry's main theme was that dried eggs, which the ration book-holder could get in the form of one 12-egg pack (price 1/3d) per four-week rationing period (that is, three eggs a week), were as wholesome, digestible and nourishing as fresh eggs. They also built muscle and repaired tissue in the same way as chops and steaks (also rationed) did. There was no need to hoard them, since there would be plenty more coming.

Using dried egg was simple. All you had to do was:

- Store packs in a cool, dry place and firmly replace the lid of the tin after use.

- Make one fresh egg by mixing one level tablespoon of the powder with two tablespoons of water, being careful to keep measurements exact.

- Treat the reconstituted egg as you would a fresh one. Use it at once, and do not make up more egg than you need for the dish you are making.

- Use dried egg dry in batters or 'rubbed-in' cake mixtures, increasing the recipe's liquid measure by 2 tablespoons for every dried egg.

As they became more practiced in their use, housewives were soon successfully scrambling dried eggs, turning them into omelettes, soufflés and batters, and making all kinds of cakes, including sponges.

67

DRIED AND IN TINS

Almost as familiar as packs of dried egg powder in the wartime kitchen were tins of dried milk. Controlled distribution of fresh liquid milk had to begin in November 1941, with everyone, except children and pregnant women who were allowed more, being allowed two to two-and-a-half pints a week. In the following month something called Household Milk went on sale. This was dried skimmed milk powder, each tin of which was equal to four pints of liquid milk, once water had been added to it. Every family was allowed one tin of Household Milk a month.

Although it was pretty undrinkable on its own – coffee, or chicory substitutes like Camp's Coffee Essence, and cocoa made it into an acceptable hot drink. Household Milk was very useful as a substitute for fresh milk in cooking and baking.

Frugal housewives also came up with a spread that could be used on top of bread or toast by filling a cup half full of powdered milk, a quarter full with sugar and a quarter full with cocoa and mixing to a paste with water.

National Dried Milk was later made available for one- and two-year-olds. This was a product based on full-cream milk and so was much nearer the real thing.

Atlantic, could earn anything up to seventeen times what a good catch would have got them before the war.

Because even freshly caught fish tended to smell rather less than fresh in the several days it often took to get from its landing port to the inland fishmonger's slab, many Food Fact recipes for fish included spices, curry powder, fresh and dried herbs, vinegar, lemon juice (or 'lemon substitute') and other flavourful ingredients. These additions became essential with snoek, which left to itself, was, like whalemeat, a memorably unpalatable fish.

The arrival of fresh-salted cod brought a welcome addition to the fishmonger's slab. It was usually the fishmonger who carried out the business of soaking the fish, for up to 48 hours, to get rid of the taste of the salt in which it had been preserved, before selling it to the housewife, who knew she had to cook it the day she bought it. As always, the Food Ministry was to the fore promoting this 'good news on the Kitchen Front – it's almost free from bone, it's easy to cook, and there's no waste. Above all – it's cheap: the maximum retail price is 9d [about 4p] per lb.' It was also a pretty unexciting fish to eat – for many it had the 'taste and texture of boiled flannlelette' – and the Food Fact recipes issued by the Ministry were full of extra flavouring ingredients, plus plenty of vegetables, of course. Even after fresh-salted cod became available, many housewives preferred to make do with tinned fish, taken from the precious kitchen stock or available on points. Nella Last, as she noted in the diary she kept for Mass Observation, could make a satisfying meal simply by opening 'a wee tin of pilchards', heating them and serving them on hot toast. 'They were only 5½d, and yet were a better meal than two cod cutlets costing at least 2 shillings.'

Even Nella was astonished at how far three soldiers made one tin of sardines go. One day, three soldiers came to the WVS mobile canteen she worked in (and cooked food for), one of them saying as he arrived at the counter, '"Nine slices of toast, a tin-opener and a fork." I felt frivolous and said, "What about a toothpick?" But he said "Nay, missus, with one tin a' sardines mashed on nine slices of toast, t'bones'll not have a chance to stick i'teeth, nor anywhere else."' Nella calculated that each soldier managed to spread one and a half sardines, mashed up, over all three of his slices of toast.

Partly as a result of the drastic reduction in imported animal feed and partly because of the change from livestock grazing to arable farming, there was a large reduction in beef

FRESH SALTED COD

Families queue outside a fishmongers for fresh salted cod, which, unlike other produce, was not rationed.

THE BRITISH HOUSEWIFE is helping to make a second front — the Kitchen Front — against Hitler. That is why we say "Medals for you, Madam."

cattle, sheep and pig numbers in Britain during the war. The value of livestock products also fell considerably as a consequence, and did not start picking up again until several years after the war was over.

Good quality meat became a treat rather than a regular feature on meal tables, replaced in part by offal and such products as Spam and corned beef, which were to become familiar parts of the meat ration. Spam, which was canned spiced ham from the United States, became a great wartime standby and, along with the sound of Vera Lynn singing 'There'll be bluebirds over the white cliffs of Dover', had a major role to play in post-war nostalgia. Spam, available on the points system rather than as part of the ration, made an excellent sandwich filling, could replace pork in 'pork' pies, and could even make a hot meal when slices of it were fried with bread.

Throughout the war, meat extracts such as Oxo cubes and Bovril – 'the concentrated essence of prime lean beef' said the Bovril ads – were used to add extra nutritional value to and enhance the flavour of vegetable soups, casseroles, and gravies.

There were many ways in which the meat ration could be eked out. Among a list of suggestions issued by the *Good Housekeeping* Institute were simple, obvious ones like serving plenty of vegetables, both root and green, at all main meals, using as much internal meat (offal) as possible, and replacing meat altogether with meals based on foods such as cheese, pulses and milk, that had much the same body-building value as meat. Less obvious were ideas like adding minced vegetables or sago to minced meat, at the rate of 2oz (60g) to 1lb (450g) mince, when using it as a filling for pasties and meat roly-poly, and adding mashed potato or minced vegetables to the minced meat used in meat cakes, baked meat loaf and similar dishes.

Using such words as 'obvious' in talking about wartime nutritional advice is to make a basic, post-war-educated mistake. The wartime working man, in particular, knew very little about nutrition. Even after three years of Ministry of Food propaganda, many British men still believed that meat was better for them than cheese and that tea was more important in their daily diet than pulses like beans or lentils. And as for trying to make plain boiled beef and carrots more interesting and nutritionally valuable for the factory worker by adding a white sauce to the dish – forget it. According to the former hotel chef now in managing a factory canteen in Birmingham, his customers 'did not understand food'.

MAKING THE MOST OF RATION COUPONS AND POINTS

Careful thrifty housewives like Nella Last were ingenious in the ways they made a little meat and other foods go a long way and contrived delicious meals out of very little. Here is Nella in November 1941, describing in her Mass Observation diary how she turned a piece of bony mutton and a kidney, bought from the butcher still wrapped in good, solid fat, into a generous meal for three, cooked slowly and wonderfully fuel-efficiently, by the dining-room fire all morning:

'My bony mutton made a lovely casserole. I first fried it and then added onion, celery, carrot and turnip [before putting it beside the fire, then] adding potatoes to it three-quarters of an hour before lunch. On the other side of the fire I had my big pan with the suet pudding in, and it really was one of the best puddings I've made for a long time. I minced the suet from the kidney… and also two slices of wholemeal bread [Nella baked her own bread] and two strips of my candied peel, made by boiling orange peel till tender in a little honey and water. I added an egg beaten in hot water, to bring it up to the quantity of the two eggs that I used to use, and then a 5½d pot of sweetened bun flour and a tablespoon of sultanas.'

Because she had no milk to make a sauce for the pudding, she contrived a sauce with custard powder mixed with water, and added honey as a sweetener. This she passed off lightly as 'a clear honey sauce for a change'. It fooled her husband, who disliked being fobbed off with what he thought of as 'economy dodge' dishes: 'By Gad, it's grand – and brings out the real flavour of the pudding.'

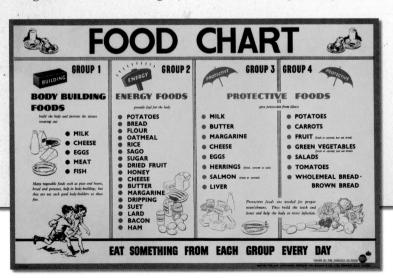

DO-IT-YOURSELF
ABOUT THE HOUSE

Historians of domestic architecture in Britain cannot point to a particular style and say 'that is a typical wartime house'. There were virtually no new houses built in Britain during World War Two. There was a lot of patching up, which, if extensive, repeated as best it could the style of the existing house, a lot of making damaged buildings habitable, and much billeting of whole families on other households, often far from the families' original home towns – thus adding to the nation's already great over-crowding problem, especially among the poorer classes.

Towards the end of the war, 'prefabs' began to appear. These were houses that were pre-fabricated in factories and were very utilitarian, being basically plain boxes with doors and windows, that could be quickly erected to provide reasonably warm and comfortable homes for bombed-out families until such time as they could be replaced by something better.

In March 1944, the Prime Minister promised, as part of the recently established Temporary Housing Programme, half a million prefabs – originally called 'Portal' homes after the Minister of Works, Lord Portal – but only about 160,000 had been completed by the war's end, most of them set on their own small plot of land on the edges of large towns and cities. Cost, plus unavailability of materials, were major reasons

for the promised half million prefabs not being built. They were surprisingly expensive to manufacture and this, plus their perceived short life-span (several models were given a life-span of only ten to fifteen years), decided hard-pressed local councils against investing in them. Many, it turned out, continued to provide perfectly adequate housing for decades after the war and into the twenty-first century.

A major social problem in the 1930s was the amount of housing in Britain that was either very below-standard, grossly over-crowded, or officially condemned – all this despite a housing policy that had led to considerable improvements in the nation's stock of housing in the 1930s. War added drastically to the amount of housing fit only to be condemned, while also destroying thousands of once per-

PREFABRICATED HOUSING
Prefabricated asbestos houses could be built in three days which made them ideal for the housing shortage during the war. These are being erected on a bombed out site at Eleanor Road, Hackney, London.

fectly good houses: by the spring of 1941, nearly a million and a half people in London alone had been made homeless by bombing.

By 1942, it was estimated that more than a million people were living in housing that, before the war, would have been condemned. Another two and a half million families were living in bomb-damaged houses that had received only essential repairs – the sort that

got the water and power back on and ensured a weatherproof roof over their occupants' heads, glass in the windows and a closable front-door.

The two main reasons for such an absence of replacement building during the war were lack of materials and lack of builders. The building materials that were available and the men qualified to use them were diverted to build camps for servicemen, hangars for aeroplanes,

STYLING THE LOW-COST PREFAB

Prefabs were bungalows – that is, they were one-floor houses, so there was no need for staircases, cellars or attics. Thirteen different designs were produced, some with flat roofs and some with just enough room under the roof for water tanks. Each design included two bedrooms and a centrally-placed, Ministry of Works-designed 'service unit' comprising kitchen, bathroom and toilet. The kitchen and bathroom were cleverly placed back to back so that their plumbing could be hidden between them. Each design also incorporated mains electricity, running hot water, built-in storage and a refrigerator.

With the exception of one American import, all the prefab designs were the work of British architects and designers. The Arcon Mark V was steel-framed and had asbestos cement panels, the asbestos making it unacceptable today. The BISF (British Iron and Steel Federation)

house was built partly in the factory and partly on site. The Tarran and Uni-Seco prefab was timber framed. The prefab expected to have the longest lifespan – at least forty years – was the aluminium one designed by the Aircraft Industries Research Organisation on Housing (AIROH). This model was made in factories that had spent most of the war in aircraft production.

Whatever their construction material, prefabs were generally liked by the people who moved into them, despite their utilitarian appearance. For people whose previous homes had been in crowded inner city terraces and tenements, many without bathrooms and with an outside toilet shared by several families, these little detached houses, sitting in their own small garden and coming complete with hot water at the turn of a tap, an indoor toilet and a refrigerator, were desirable indeed.

factories for war industries and everything else needed to meet the complex requirements of a country on a total war footing. It was not until early 1943 that the War Cabinet agreed to moving men and materials to the work of repairing the thousands of houses made uninhabitable by bombing. In early 1944 that

the government told local authorities that they could start using plant and machinery from airfield construction sites as they became available to prepare sites for new housing, with the necessary services.

In the meantime, much of the work of making bomb-damaged houses habitable again had fallen on the houses' owners and occupiers. In December 1940, when the Blitz was reaching a climax of horror and devastation, the Ministry of Home Security issued a leaflet called 'After the Raid' in which it set out the compensation householders could expect to receive, and gave the number of the form – VOW 1 – that owners and long-term occupiers of damaged or destroyed houses would have to fill in to get it: 'The amount of your compensation and the time of paying it will depend on the passing of the War Damage Bill now before Parliament. 'If your house can be made fit to live in with a few simple repairs the local authority will put it right if the landlord is not able to do it. But how quickly the local authority can do this depends on local conditions.'

Since, it has been estimated, between a third and a fifth of all houses in the country suffered some sort of damage during the war, 'local conditions' could cover a wide range of interpretations. And the monetary compensation could take a long time to come through – 'unless you are in financial difficulties, [not until] after the war has ceased' thought the author of *War Time Household Repairs*, published by the *Daily Express* newspaper.

War Time Household Repairs also pointed out that most houses damaged during an air raid were 'made uncomfortable rather than dangerous' and could be made habitable by a 'handy person' – such as the readers of the *Daily Express*, most of whom had practiced 'do-it-yourself' to a greater or lesser degree during the 1920s and 1930s. The great thing about temporary repairs was that they were best done using whatever was to hand, and not buying new materials, said the carefully cheerful author of *War Time Household Repairs*,

BEYOND REPAIR
Many houses were beyond repair and the demolition squad had to come in and clear the debris.

knowing full well that new materials were almost impossible to get.

What might 'uncomfortable rather than dangerous' mean? It could mean that when you crawled out of your Morrison shelter or the understairs cupboard or the Anderson shelter in the garden, you found that many of the tiles had been blown off your roof, many of the windows had no glass in them, a door or two

INSULATING TIPS

Today, we may not need to stretch cellophane across windows to protect ourselves from glass splinters, but the concept of covering windows with various materials is a useful one.

- If you do not have the luxury of central heating, you can buy a kit from a DIY store to stop the heat escaping through the glass. The kit contains heat-shrinkable plastic and some adhesive tape. You simply tape the plastic snugly inside your window frame and then shrink it using the heat from a hair dryer. This will make it perfectly tight and as clear as the glass in the window. In the springtime, when you no longer need the insulation, simply peel off the tape and throw it away.
- Heavy curtains at your windows and exterior doors will help the draughts from chilling your rooms.
- Apply weatherstripping around doors and windows that are draughty. Make sure the surface is clean and dry before applying the weatherstripping, and it is best to put it on in temperatures above 20°F (−6°C).

might have been splintered or blown off their hinges, there might be cracks or large holes in the ceiling plaster, and over and in everything would be a layer of dust, including soot and ash blown down the chimney, that would take weeks to get rid of.

For many householders, it was very much a question of making do with makeshift arrangements. For instance, if all the tarpaulins stored in the nearest air raid wardens' post had already been taken, the householder could perhaps tie a canvas tent over the holes in his roof where tiles had been blown off or bombs fallen through. This would at least keep the rain out until the council's workmen got to you with replacement tiles. Windows could be covered with cardboard or scraps of wood until the council's glaziers could get to your house with some precious, increasingly difficult to obtain, window glazing.

Schoolboy Derek Lambert, returning to London from a holiday by the sea in Devon (or as near the sea as he could get for the barbed wire and scaffolding invasion defences) was met by his mother saying she was afraid his room was in an awful mess. 'We've been bombed, you see.' The bomb had fallen close enough to their house to take the tiles off the roof, shake down ceilings and blow out some of the windows. 'Ceilings made of hard-board replaced the plaster and stayed there until the end of the war,' Derek recalled in his wartime memoir *The Sheltered Days*.

On the positive side, electricity was usually restored in a few hours and piped water within days of a bombing raid. Housewives might only have to cook a meal or two on an open fire (often fuelled by wood from bombed houses) and collect water in buckets from an army lorry or a standpipe for two or three days. If the local baker's oven had been spared, then he would cook all the Sunday joints and casseroles of the neighbourhood in it.

In the absence of new wallpaper, many people turned to paint and distemper to give their walls a new look – not that there was a great range of paints to choose from, since every colour except the standard boring institutional creams, greens and browns disappeared very early. Ceiling whitening, still available, could be coloured with dyes and used as a wall paint, often over existing old and faded wallpaper. A different coloured paint applied over the base coat with a sponge produced a good-looking stippled effect – an effect which had a comeback in the 1980s.

The average wartime house was made

PROTECTING FROM SPLINTERS

A useful tip that many householders and office workers used, was to apply cellophane to the glass in their windows to protect themselves from glass splinters during an air raid.

CAREFULLY CONSERVING WALLPAPER

The production of wallpaper virtually ceased during the war, putting a premium on old stocks in warehouses, or rolls left in attics after some home do-it-yourself. Sometimes after an air raid, wallpaper came away from walls in such a way that it could be put back – provided one could obtain wallpaper paste. In 1940, manufacturers helped the householder by introducing specially prepared packs of a dry adhesive that needed just the addition of cold water to become an effective paste. Among the hints for cleaning or repairing wallpaper that appeared in wartime women's magazines were:

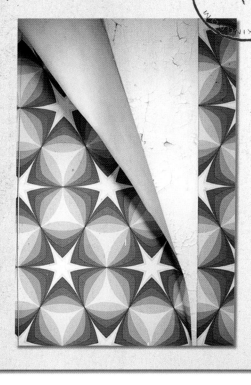

- If the wallpaper is washable (test an area behind a picture or mirror), dab it with just a small amount of clean water (no soap).

- Clean non-washable paper with day-old bread (stale enough not to crumble), or with an India rubber.

- Remove grease spots and marks with benzine, painted on with a soft brush and any excess blotted off.

- Use waterpaint, carefully mixed so that it matches the wallpaper, to paint over scratches.

- If there are holes in the plaster beneath a section of wallpaper, carefully peel it back and fill the hole with Keene's cement; wait until the cement is dry before pasting back the wallpaper.

- Always keep all wallpaper, including off-cuts and strips, left over from a do-it-yourself job. You may need them for patching damaged paper.

distinctly shabby by the lack of paints, wall-papers, plaster, screws and nails, plumbing, electrical bits and pieces and other DIY materials. So shabby were some of the houses that American servicemen, arriving in the UK in force during 1942, were warned not to show surprise at or to comment on the state of British homes.

During the 1930s many newspapers, as part of their on-going circulation wars, published a wide range of do-it-yourself and make-do-and-mend books, and continued to do so during the war. One rather ill-timed publication was the *News Chronicle's Modern Make Do and Mend*, which covered most of the minor repairs a wartime householder would have to deal with. Published in 1939, it would probably have been shelved if its editors had realized how scarce the mending materials it advocated would soon become.

Two areas in which do-it-yourself took on greater financial significance in the wartime house than in the inter-war period were the provision of fuel and the business of getting the household laundry done. According to *Good Housekeeping* magazine, which early in the war published an article on how the British housewife could 'budget for Victory', 'laundrywork' and 'fuel – coal, gas and electricity' were two of the most expensive items in the weekly household budget.

Of the three kinds of fuel, electricity was considered to be the fuel that could be most effectively used in the battle on the Home Front. Electricity was sold for decades before the war as the up-to-date, clean and efficient way to power the modern home. Minor

REPLACING A FUSE

Many women were left to bring up their family alone while their men fought to save their country and it helped if they knew a little DIY to keep the home running smoothly. Today many women choose to live on their own, so learning the basics has become a necessity rather than a luxury if they don't want to rely entirely on the local handyman.

- If your electrical appliance has stopped working, the chances are that the fuse has blown. Plugs will be fitted with either a 13amp or 3amp fuse depending on the appliance. Check the underside of the appliance for its wattage, anything over 700W will require a 13amp fuse.
- Unplug the appliance and unscrew the cover.
- Remove the old fuse cartridge from its holder and replace with a new one of the same ampage.

If your appliance still doesn't work, then the chances are one of the wires has come loose and you will need to check that they are all in their correct terminals. Blue goes to Neutral; Brown to Live and Green-and-Yellow to Earth. Once the wires are firmly secured, replace the cover and screw together.

HIDING THE LIGHT

The street lights were turned off at night and there had to be thick curtains, lined with blackout material at the windows so that no chink of light would show through.

electrical repairs and maintenance, such as changing fuses and rewiring light bulbs, became a basic of the do-it-yourself revolution, in which the housewife was as much involved as her husband.

With the war, the emphasis as far as electricity was concerned was all on making the best use of it while reducing the amount one used. The Electrical Association for Women (EWA) changed the contents of its pamphlets and booklets from using electricity in the home and successfully making minor electrical repairs to saving energy, using electrical gadgets less than before and cooking fuel-efficiently with electricity. As for the cook in the kitchen, advice and help went beyond the simple use of food, both rationed and non-rationed. If they could get them, many housewives used half moon-shaped saucepans, two of which could be fitted together on one hob (or gas ring), and heeded all the advice about not wasting fuel by over-cooking foods and then keeping them hot in the oven.

Keeping up with the family laundry presented many problems for the wartime housewife. It was all very well for *Good House-keeping* to recommend that the housewife should now aim to save energy by reducing her weekly laundry bill by a third [from 10 shillings to 7 shillings], perhaps by sending large items, such as 'sheets, table-cloths, large bath towels and possibly men's shirts' to the laundry while washing the 'smalls' at home. But the fact was that many laundries soon closed completely, their staff having disappeared into war work, others put up their prices and others closed their lists to new customers.

Electric washing machines, although made

BLACKOUT CURTAINS

Having to cover every source of light in the evening and blackout every window is believed to be one of the main irritations of the wartime housewife, but this trick of making a room completely dark is a good one, and can aid a good nights sleep. To get the blackout effect you will need: measuring tape, curtain fabric, matching thread, blackout backing, scissors, pins, sewing machine, curtain road, work surface, iron and ironing board.

1 Install the curtain rod above the window.
2 Measure the distance between the top of the curtain rod to where you want the curtains to finish.
3 Buy the amount of fabric you need and an equal amount of blackout backing.
4 Lay the curtain fabric right side down on your work surface. Spread the blackout backing right side up on the curtain. Position the blackout backing so you have 1½ inches of extra fabric on each side.
5 Fold one edge of the curtain fabric over ¾ inch, so the cut edge of the curtain is even with the edge of the blackout backing. Then fold the curtain fabric another ¾ inch, so it is over the edge of the blackout backing.

6 Secure the folded edge in place with pins and then stitch.
7 Repeat step 5 and 6 for the other edges of the curtain fabric.
8 Fold the top edge of the curtain over 4 inches towards the blackout backing, ensure this is even. Pin and stitch in place.
9 Insert the curtain rod through the fold you have just created.

THE UNITED KINGDOM
THRIFTY TIP
THE UNITED KINGDOM

LIGHTING THE HOUSE IN THE BLACKOUT

The wartime blackout was, for many, the greatest inconvenience and irritation of the war. Although the blackout meant that no lights inside the house could be seen from the outside, this did not mean that domestic lighting had to be very dim, even though everyone was asked to use low-wattage light bulbs, and to use the newly available black or dark blue painted blackout bulbs. Also available were light fittings with bayonet fixtures able to take torch bulbs, that could be plugged into a normal light. The torch bulbs, being unreflected because they were not in a torch, helped reduce the darkness of halls, passageways and landings without throwing a bright light.

There were disadvantages, of course, not the least being that torch bulbs and batteries became very scarce within weeks of the war starting. Then there was the increased likelihood of accidents around the dimly lit home, if too many low-wattage light bulbs replaced stronger ones or too many paper shades or cardboard boxes were used to dim bare bulbs. Rather than black out all windows, particularly those in bedrooms, many people preferred to undress in the dark and go to bed in the dark. Manufacturers like G.E.C. were soon recommending the sensible rather than extravagant use of its light bulbs behind the blacked-out and heavily curtained windows of the wartime house to prevent accidents and help preserve eyesight, too: 'Electric light is cheap. Better light – better sight'. G.E.C. and other light bulb manufacturers entered fully into wartime salvage schemes, even printing the wrapping paper round light bulbs with reminders to put the used wrappers in the paper salvage box.

It was not until September 1944 that the strict blackout regulations – infringement of which had led to 925,000 people being prosecuted in the courts – were relaxed, with a 'dim-out' being allowed in its place. Many householders left their blackout material in place – just in case.

in Britain and used in many homes, were not seen as valuable a domestic aid as, for instance, the vacuum cleaner – and anyway their manufacture was abruptly stopped with the war. Many housewives did not send out their washing to the local laundry and chose to continue to use a washing tub, which might be just a simple tub with a wooden washing board in it, or it could be a double tub, with a wringer set up between the two tubs and which was kept in the scullery.

For all women, soap rationing, when it was imposed in February 1942, at the amount of 16 ounces (450g) every four weeks, came almost

ALL HANDS TO THE MANGLE

To make washday less of a chore, mother often involved the children. For those families without the luxury of a washing machine, washing by hand and squeezing water out with a mangle could take up a whole day.

THE MANY USES OF WASHING SODA

Washing soda, properly diluted, had many cleaning uses in the home, especially in the kitchen and scullery.

- Used once a week in a strong solution, washing soda kept the kitchen sink clean and its drain pipe free of grease. The modern gas or electric cooker also benefited from a weekly clean with hot soda water. The meat safe could be made hygienically clean and grease-free by washing it every week with hot soda water, thoroughly rinsing it and, ideally, placing it out-of-doors to dry thoroughly.

- Washing soda was used in milder solutions as a water softener for laundry, unless really greasy work clothes were involved, when a preliminary soak in a stronger soda solution was needed. Softening the water meant that less soap was needed, so that the precious soap ration was saved.

- The recommended solution was 1oz (30g) of washing soda dissolved in 1 pint (600ml) of water. This solution was kept in a bottle and used at the rate of 1 tablespoon to every gallon of hot water for every 5 degrees of hardness in the water. (It was up to the housewife to check the degree of hardness of the local water with her water company.) The solution was added to hot water before the soap was added.

as the last straw. Many long-favoured cleaning products had been disappearing from shop shelves for months, if not years, but for the basic laundry cleaner – soap – to be obtainable only with ration coupons seemed hard indeed, even if the allowance was carefully apportioned between laundry soap flakes, laundry soap, soap powder and toilet soap.

From now on, the wartime housewife's household cleaners were much the same materials as her grandmothers and great-grandmothers had used: soap, washing soda, salt, ammonia, bleach

THRIFTY TIP
THE UNITED KINGDOM THE UNITED KINGDOM

NATURAL LAUNDRY

Natural cleaning products are as popular now as they were during the war. Lemon, salt, vinegar and bicarbonate of soda can all be used to clean and deodorise as an alternative to expensive, artificial, pollutant products.

- Adding lemon juice in with your laundry may seem odd, but it works in many natural ways – bleaching out stains such as ink and fruit juice, as well as brightening whites and leaving a subtle, fresh fragrance.
- Boiling soiled cottons or linens in a salt and bicarbonate of soda solution can restore items to their original white.
- Odd stockings of different shades will come out matching if boiled in salty water.
- Use white vinegar in place of fabric softener.

DUAL TUB

For those housewives lucky enough to be able to afford one, the new British dual tub allowed you to do both your laundry and your washing up by simply exchanging the drum.

and vinegar, and also rainwater, a naturally soft water. Even starching her table-linen was a problem for the houseproud women, because the best substitutes for laundry starch were such farinaceous substances as flour, cornflour and rice water, all of which were now vital wartime foods.

One of the biggest elements of the wartime laundry revolution was the recommendation to give clothes a preliminary soak before washing and thus do away with the need to boil them, a washing method that wasted precious fuel. White linens such as bed linen, which boiling kept white, were helped to retain their whiteness when not boiled by putting 'blue', or dolly blue, in the final rinsing water. The best quality blue was block blue, which came in a muslin bag which was swished around in the water before the clothes were added.

MAKING A HOME
IN WARTIME

The austerity that reigned in wartime Britain was nowhere felt more severely than in the home. Obtaining even the simplest basic, like a new frying pan or a bed sheet, was made hugely difficult, if not impossible, by a series of government control orders that either prohibited production of certain articles altogether, cut production figures, or rigorously controlled the amount and quality of materials that could be produced. Items from tables and chairs, cups and saucers, saucepans and cutlery to electrical goods, curtains, carpets and rugs were hard to obtain.

For most families in Britain, already in their own fully furnished and equipped homes at the outbreak of war and remaining well away from what the government called the 'danger areas', the war became a time of austerity rather than danger. They were not bombed out of their houses, they did not suffer so much as a broken window or a lost roof tile. What people put up with, generally without complaint and with a resigned shrug, was an inability to replace with something new any of those household items that get worn, damaged or broken in the ordinary course of domestic life.

Unless you were bombed out or were about to marry and start your first home, there was very little chance of your getting new furniture during the war – and for a full eight years after it. Second-hand furniture also became both hard to get and prohibitively expensive as the war went on. Pieces of furniture like plain oak tables, which might have fetched £4 at auction before the war, were selling for six or seven times that amount, even in country auction sales, by 1943.

The main problem about furniture in wartime was, as with so much else, a lack of the materials needed for it allied, of course, to a lack of workers to make it and factories to make it in. Almost the first measure brought in by the government after war was declared in 1939 was a Control of Timber Order, issued by the Ministry of Supply on 5 September. This was necessary to conserve stocks of timber, a vital war material imports of which would now be severely cut, if not lost altogether in the face of U-boat attacks in the Atlantic and enemy action in the Baltic region, where much of Britain's imported timber came from. The Control of

A BOARD OF TRADE HOUSEHOLD CONVERSION TABLE

The Board of Trade issued many leaflets in its effort to justify and explain its many limitation of supplies and control orders. This leaflet, suggesting as it does some very unlikely conversions, is perhaps not typical of them.

IN WARTIME, production must be for war and not for peace, began the leaflet's text. Among the examples of peacetime items which would now have to be changed over to wartime necessities, the leaflet went on, were several familiar, even basic, household items:

LACE CURTAINS become Sand-fly Netting

CARPETS become Webbing Equipment

TOILET PREPARATIONS become Anti-Gas Ointments

MATTRESSES become Life Jackets

SAUCEPANS become Steel Helmets.

Timber Order was also a sign – if such a sign were needed – that during this war the state would have total control over the supply of all scarce materials.

The Control of Timber Order limited supplies to a list of approved manufacturers only, who were limited to their existing pre-war stocks. They would be using it to make, not much domestic furniture – unless bunk beds for air-raid shelters could be classified as 'domestic' – but mostly everything wooden needed by the armed services from rifle butts and ammunition cases to RAF huts and military desks and chairs. In July 1940, just months before the Blitz began, the supply of timber for domestic furniture was cut completely, leaving some pre-war timber to make small quantities of replacement furniture for distributing among the bombed-out. There would be no more timber for domestic furniture until April 1941.

As the bombing went on, many local authorities gathered together stores of second-hand furniture for meeting the immediate needs of bombed-out families. Quite a lot of this furniture was rescued from bombed houses by council salvage squads – if looters had not risked life and limb to get it first. If salvaged furniture was not claimed by its owners, it was added to the council's store and was lent free to bombed-out families for three months, at the

WASTE NOT WANT NOT
Old doors are reused as bed-heads, steel tubing is the framework and canvas the mattress for bunk beds in this London air raid shelter.

end of which time they could either return it or buy it.

The government's first move towards meeting the increasingly desperate need for furniture came in February 1941 with the development of a range of cheap and rather shoddy Standard Emergency Furniture. But it was a step in the right direction, and Standard

Emergency Furniture provided the starting point for the much better – and more enduring – Utility furniture. This quickly followed the Board of Trade's first venture into well-designed standardisation, Utility clothing, launched in the spring of 1942.

As with Utility clothing, so with Utility furniture, the government, through the Board of Trade, controlled not just the availability of timber to make it, but also its design and the price at which it could be sold. In May 1942, the government issued a Furniture (Maximum Prices) Order which covered both new and second-hand furniture and followed this up in July with an Advisory Committee on Utility Furniture, set up by the President of the Board of Trade, Hugh Dalton.

Also as with Utility clothing, the best designers available were put on to the nine-man Advisory Committee, including the leading designers Charles Tennyson and Gordon Russell, the domestic architecture historian John Gloag and two representatives of the ordinary consumer, a vicar and a housewife. This committee was charged with the task of overseeing the production of furniture 'of sound construction and maximum economy of labour and materials'.

The furniture should be simple in design and construction, displaying a fine fitness for purpose – a favourite mantra with progressive designers in the 1930s. There was to be nothing shoddy about its production – for instance, all joints were to be morticed or pegged, screws rather than pins were to be used, and there were to be no plastic fittings, because plastic was an essential war material. Careful choice of design and strict adherence to the wartime 'waste not want not' mantra led to the fabrics used in

GIVE IT A NEW LOOK

THRIFTY TIP

The wartime mentality of 'make do and mend' teaches us not to be wasteful of material goods, and that altering, customising or fixing our possessions can be satisfying on the conscience and bank balance.

- Reinvent dull-looking furniture with a fresh coat of paint.

- If paint supplies are limited but your magnolia bedroom is driving you mad, paint just one wall a striking colour.

- Stencil characters or pictures on your child's bedroom walls as an alternative to expensive character-themed wallpaper.

- Sand down old wooden furniture to give it a new look.

- Make new cushion covers out of old curtains or dress fabric to jazz up a sofa.

- If you are bored with curtains why not make some ornate tie-backs and hook them back during the day.

- If you want to change the colour of your furniture but money is tight, why not use some bright coloured throws.

A UTILITY BEDROOM
This wartime bedroom consists of two simple pieces of utility furniture, a bed and a tallboy.

Utility furniture all being designed with small repeat patterns, ensuring very little wastage, in a limited colour range – natural (cream), green, blue, and rust – and in light fabric weights.

The results of the committee's work were first seen in an exhibition set up in the Building Centre in London in October 1942. The exhibition was opened by Hugh Dalton, President of the Board of Trade – a sign of the importance the government attached to the Utility scheme. Three months later, in January

1943, the first twenty Utility furniture designs went on sale. Each article of furniture came in two qualities of material used and, usually, in three designs. Shop-keepers were ordered to sell by the end of February any non-Utility furniture they might still have in stock.

A limited range of hardwoods, especially oak but also mahogany, plus veneered hardboard rather than plywood (an essential material in aircraft manufacture) for back panels and the like, was set aside for Utility furniture. Large items like settees, which would have required an unacceptable number of steel springs, were absent from the first range of twenty pieces of Utility furniture, which included wooden-framed armchairs, sideboards, kitchen chairs, beds and kitchen tables.

Utility furniture was made by 72 licensed manufacturers, working in 150 factories in Britain and giving jobs to about 5000 workers. In the first two months after the scheme was launched, some 25,000 units of Utility furniture were issued to eager buyers. All pieces of Utility furniture were stamped with the soon-to-be very familiar Utility mark, 'CC41'.

The first Utility furniture was generally well received. While Utility furniture could not match the best Art Deco and Modernist furniture design of the 1930s, with its tubular steel construction and moulded plywood frames, this wartime economy furniture

IMPROVISATION

For those families who had lost a lot of furniture, improvisation was the only answer.

UTILITY FURNITURE – A COMPLICATED BUY

The first catalogue of Utility Furniture came as a New Year's gift for all potential brides and grooms as it was published on New Year's Day, 1943. Actually obtaining any of the simple, even restrainedly elegant pieces of furniture in the catalogue would not be a simple matter of choosing what you wanted and then adding them to your wedding presents list.

To begin with, you had to prove that you were eligible for the Units that you needed to be able to buy Utility furniture in the first place. Being about to be married, newly married, or having been bombed-out, were the main criteria for eligibility, and it also helped that a married couple were about to start a family. You got your application form from the local Fuel Office and, when completed, submitted it to the local Assistance Board.

The Assistance Board issued you with a Buying Permit, which contained a specific number of Utility Furniture Units – sixty in the first Permit booklet and considerably reduced thereafter. These were not enough to allow you to buy everything you would need to furnish a new home, so you would be making a very careful choice. If you were allocated a total of 25 or 30 Units, you would be unlikely to buy both a dressing table (8 Units) and a tallboy (also 8 Units) when you really needed a wardrobe (10 or 12 Units, depending on size).

The Buying Permit covered a specified Area of Validity, limiting it to a shop within a 15-mile radius of the address to which the furniture was to be delivered.

The Buying Permit also contained the Priority Dockets you had been allocated for the purchase of such essential new home extras as curtain material, floor covering, mattresses, blankets and sheets. You were unlikely to get a tick beside every one of the Priority Dockets listed, and specific quantities – 15 square yards of curtain material, 20 square yards of linoleum, or 12 sheets, for instance – would be included on the Dockets themselves.

was clearly well built and simply designed – obviously of better quality than most of the mid-range furniture that had been made in Britain during the 1930s. It also seemed good to those visiting the exhibition that fair prices had been set on the Utility furniture.

While Utility furniture was fine by most of those who were obtaining it to replace what they had lost when their homes had been destroyed, a few modern young brides-to-be were less enthusiastic. There were half a million marriages in Britain every year during the war, which meant that there were also up to half a million brides a year hoping to start married life with a home of their own, and with new furniture in it.

Maggie Blunt, a writer and assistant on an architectural journal, confided to the diary she kept for Mass Observation that her recently engaged friends Meg and Roger were finding that furniture, which had become either very expensive or simply unobtainable, was the major difficulty in their plans for setting up a new home. Meg wanted everything to be ultra-modern – no doubt with tubular steel frames, stylish Art Deco fabric designs and smoothly curved moulded plywood to the fore – whereas her fiancé favoured old oak and copper. Neither had much hope of getting what they liked in 1943.

'I think [Meg] is influenced by highbrow critics in architectural and art press,' sighed Maggie Blunt in her diary in March 1943. 'I saw [Utility furniture] in the Building Centre and thought it might have been much worse… if Meg had seen some of it in Bowmans before the war she would have chosen it without hesitation.' When Meg, 'radiant in powder blue and navy accessories', and Roger were married

HOW TO MAKE A RAG RUG

GET EXCITED AND MAKE THINGS

THRIFTY TIP

You can use most kinds of fabric to make colourful rag rugs, as long as you can cut it into strips and it will stand the wear and tear. There are many different methods but this one is the 'hooking' version made on canvas with a large crochet hook, or latchet hook.

- First draw your shape on a piece of canvas in felt tip pen.
- Work out your pattern on a piece of paper or just work randomly with your chosen fabric pieces.
- Cut or tear strips from your chosen fabric and relax in the evening by hooking them through the canvas.
- Braided rugs are made from long plaits of material wound into rounds or ovals. This type of rug is very hardwearing.

in June, they were well aware that making a matrimonial home in wartime was not going to be easy.

As Maggie Blunt noted, the housing shortage by now was acute, furniture was scarce and expensive, there was little domestic ware available, only very limited supplies of crockery and cutlery and brides needed coupons for furnishing fabrics and linens.

Although crockery was not rationed during the war, its production was severely limited, with decoration and time-consuming floral patterns on pottery actually being banned in February 1942. In early summer 1942, by which time current supplies of crockery were an estimated one hundred million pieces below minimum needs, the government banned the production of all but a narrow range of simple

EMERGENCY BEDDING

The home of the Foreign Secretary Viscount Halifax at 88 Easton Square, London, became the emergency centre for clothing, bedding and crockery, manned by members of the WVS.

NEW LIFE FOR OLD SHEETS

Good Housekeeping's 1943 advice on looking after sheets was clear and precise. It began with a recommendation that every housewife should keep a close eye on her bed linen so that she could deal with any wear and tear before it became irreparable: there was little chance of it being replaced with anything new until the war was over.

A sheet worn in the middle could easily be given several more years of good use:

- First step – cut your sheet in half lengthways down the centre and join the selvedges by hand in a flat seam.

- Machine-stitch the outer edges [now the thin parts of the sheet]. These thin parts will go under the mattress where there's little strain on them, so your re-made sheet is almost as strong as when new.

The Board of Trade's own sheet-care leaflet advised women not to iron folds into the sheets, as this caused unnecessary wear.

THRIFTY TIP

NEW LIFE for old SHEETS

FIRST STEP — TEAR YOUR WORN SHEET DOWN THE CENTRE

Watch for signs of wear and deal with a sheet that needs it before there's a hole. Tear or cut it in half lengthwise and join the selvedges in a flat seam by hand. Then machine-hem the outer edges. These thin parts will go under the mattress where there's little strain on them, so your re-made sheet is almost as strong as when new.

Not only sheets but *all* your household things must be made the very most of. These hints will help you to put off buying new.

USE SHEETS AND PILLOWCASES TURN AND TURN ABOUT, so that each gets its fair share of wear. Put newly laundered ones on top of the pile and take them out from underneath. Things not in constant use should not be stored in a hot cupboard as heat weakens the material. Save wear and tear by mending things that need it before they are washed, or at least by giving them "first-aid tacking." When the washing is done at home, avoid bleaching (which is an expert's job) or you may damage your things. Dry in the sun instead wherever possible. In ironing, take care the iron isn't too hot and never iron over the folds. Air everything thoroughly.

See to Stains at once. Practically all stains will come out if treated at once. Pour boiling water through tea and coffee stains while wet, then wash in the usual way—do the same with fruit stains. Don't forget that egg stains and blood stains should be soaked in *cold* water.

Things you can turn into Towels. A most serviceable bath towel can be made out of an old honeycomb bedspread that you are no longer using. Tea towels can often be made out of worn table runners, table mats, doyleys, etc., otherwise they should be put by for the duration to save laundering and mending. Never let things get too dirty before washing them: the extra rubbing is harmful and you use more soap in the end. Watch your towels for thin places and mend before holes come and before washing. When patches are needed, use old material—a new patch on a worn towel is apt to tear away. Two thin towels diamond-stitched together will make one strong one. Towels don't need to be ironed—rough drying will save time and wear.

Mend and Make-do to save buying new

HONEY CAKE

---·····●●●●●●●·····---

112 g butter or margarine
250 ml runny honey
1 egg, well beaten
250 g self-raising flour
1 tsp bicarbonate of soda
½ teaspoon salt
½ teaspoon ground cinnamon
125 ml sour milk (or 125 ml milk mixed with
    ½ teaspoon white vinegar)
75 g chopped nuts

- Preheat the oven to 350°F/180°C/Gas
  mark 4. Grease and flour a 13 x 9 in
  baking tin.

- Cream the butter or margarine in a
  large bowl, then add the beaten egg and
  honey.

- In a second bowl, sift together the
  bicarbonate of soda, flour, salt and
  cinnamon.

- Add alternately with the sour milk to
  the creamed butter mixture. Add the
  nuts.

- This should resemble a batter. Pour
  into the prepared baking tin and bake
  in preheated oven for 35 minutes or
  until done. Test by inserting a skewer or
  knife into the centre, this will come out
  clean when the cake is cooked.

white domestic pottery; a small amount of the fine china that England was famous for was allowed for the transatlantic trade.

The government was not unaware of these difficulties. At the Utility furniture exhibition in London in October 1942, the Board of Trade had also displayed some of the new-style crockery being made by companies like Wedgwood. The pottery shown on the Utility kitchen table was plain white and simply designed. Some of the pieces were designed for double use. Many cups were designed without handles (a materials-saving ploy) and one could be turned into a jam pot by simply putting the lid of the teapot on it – always assuming that the teapot was not itself being used.

The truth was, that it was the government itself that had done most to make domestic ware so little available. As part of its major effort to divert raw materials and workers to war industry, the government brought in a Limitations of Supply Order in June 1940 which was aimed largely at the domestic consumer goods market. Among the seventeen classes of goods whose production was drastically cut back to two-thirds of the 1939 level were domestic cutlery, pottery and glassware, except for very simple jugs, mugs and tumblers. A side-effect of this order was to send prices for the goods now limited spiralling upwards. Another side effect was the use of jam jars in place of beer mugs in some pubs and many homes.

New kitchen ware was also so scarce that many brides started married life with just one saucepan in their kitchen, while their mothers seriously regretted the enthusiasm with which they had given their aluminium saucepans to Lord Beaverbrook's Spitfire Fund in 1940.

Here, again, the government was largely responsible for the lack of kitchen ware. From the autumn of 1941, the Board of Trade had been licensing all 'hollow-ware' production, including pots and pans, kettles, buckets (kept filled with water in many homes in readiness for putting out fires from incendiary bombs) and even galvanised baths (essential in the many working-class and poor homes which could not boast a bathroom).

Licences for producing hollow-ware were only given to those manufacturers who agreed to cut styles and designs to the minimally simple. Production targets were also cut so drastically that, as a Board of Trade survey discovered in 1943, only one in four women who had tried to buy a frying pan in the previous month had managed to do so. The public was indeed, as the Board of Trade admitted, being subjected to 'considerable inconvenience and difficulty' – and was also wasting time, getting tired and wearing out shoe leather going from shop to shop, none of which was good for morale.

Another area of huge difficulty for the housewife was in keeping her home properly provided with floor coverings, soft furnishings, including curtains, and bed linen. Furnishing textiles and carpets and rugs were all included in some sort of government production – or non-production – order. Rug-making, often using scraps of fabric, unravelled woollen knitwear and even old stockings woven on to a piece of sacking or hessian, became a popular pastime during the war, while many unlikely fabrics were used for curtains, cushions and chair covers.

A popular curtain fabric was the fabric bags that flour and sugar came in. They could be

FLOUR BAGS
Because fabric was so hard to come by during the war years, the bags that flour came in was bleached, dyed, unstitched and made into a wide range of household essentials.

unstitched, bleached and dyed and then made into a wide range of household essentials, including curtains, cushion covers and tea towels – the latter having been rationed, along with towels, in October 1942. Bed sheets, made only in cotton, not linen, during the war, were also virtually unobtainable without a Priority Docket. Housewives were given plenty of advice, both in their magazines and by the Board of Trade, on how to take care of their

bed linen to ensure that it would last 'for the duration'.

Perhaps to prevent householders' morale sinking to rock bottom during the war, the Board of Trade and other organisations regularly put on exhibitions that looked towards 'the home of the future'. In January 1944, the British Colour Council, 'in anticipation of the time after the war when setting up home may be a brighter process than is possible under present restrictions', as *The Times* put it, filled the galleries of the Royal Academy in London with an exhibition on 'Colour in the Home'. There were displays of colourful dining, sitting, nursery and bedroom settings and some wonderfully coloured pottery, kitchen ware and decorating materials such as paint. There were even a few suggestions for interior decoration in civil aircraft.

It would be some years before any of this made a material difference to the average home in Britain. Furniture rationing did not end until the summer of 1948, and Utility furniture itself was phased out only in 1953, the year of Elizabeth II's Coronation.

NOTHING GOES TO WASTE
Women became adept at using every scrap of fabric they had to make useful items such as aprons, shoe and stocking tidies and all without having to use any ration coupons.

HOME CARE AND MAINTENANCE

We've already noticed some ingenious ways of filling gaps in household essentials, such as jam jars for drinking vessels. Here are a few more.

The first Utility furniture range included a small set of book shelves (open-backed, so it was not a book case) which cost £1 12 shillings and required several Utility Furniture units. A near equivalent could be made out of a couple of apple boxes, stacked one on top of the other. Stacks of bricks, picked up on bomb sites, needed a couple of planks of wood to become book shelves.

Furniture and wooden floors could be polished (and their surfaces protected) with a polish made from a mixture of melted candles and beeswax.

Black-leading for stoves and fireplaces was replaced by more than one housewife by a blacking made from crushed used batteries, and brass and copper ware could be cleaned with vinegar in which salt had been dissolved.

White tablecloths were often made into sheets, and, conversely, lace bed covers could make smart curtains.

A blanket worn thin in the middle could be given a new lease of life by having a square of flannelette machine-stitched to the middle in a 'quilting' pattern.

The pieces of fabric in tailors' sample books were used – not by the housewife on her own so much as by groups of housewives in their WVS meeting room – to make bedcovers. As Nella Last noted in her Mass Observation diary, the ones she made averaged about 'seventy-seven yards of machining to join each piece with a double row of stitching and a double-stitched hem'.

Anyone with hens in the back garden was careful to keep the fabric bags in which chicken meal was sold. Unpicked, washed and perhaps dyed, they made good cushion covers.

WARDROBE
MAKE DO AND MEND

The wartime 'Make Do and Mend' slogan – as famous as 'Dig for Victory' – was first heard in Britain in the 1930s. The aftermath of the Great Recession saw a great rise in the number of householders doing all kinds of household maintenance and repair work themselves.

They were guided in their work by such publications as the *News Chronicle* newspaper's *Modern Make and Mend*. This splendid book, published in 1939, dealt with all manner of minor repairs, from dealing with faulty ball-cocks and repairing cracks in the plaster to repairing wallpaper.

The war put an end to large-scale 'do-it-yourself' work since the necessary materials were simply not available. Instead, 'Make Do and Mend' became the great wartime mantra for the housewife and mother struggling, not just with plumbing and plastering, curtains and sheets, but with the often dispiriting business of clothing herself and her family. She knew early on in the war, even before publication of the big Limitation of Supplies Order, with its ominous reference to domestic 'textiles', in June 1940, that clothing was going to be a problem.

She was right. Clothing was officially rationed, with immediate effect, on 1 June 1941. A main reason for bringing in such rationing lay in the fact that in pre-war Britain most of the nation's clothes were made at home, by a large number of small firms employing some half a million workers in many small factories. Now that the country was at war, those factories and the people who worked in them would have to be moved into the munitions industries.

Even so, many members of the government, particularly the Prime Minster, Winston

OPPOSITE: RECYCLED SCARVES
Because of rationing, women were keen to get their hands on any items that could help improve their looks. These women are buying scarves which are made out of recycled escape maps.

MAKING DO

Go through your wardrobe

Updating your existing wardrobe by customising your clothes can express your individuality and creativity. For the more adept, altering the size or shape of a garment can breathe new life into a tired outfit. Easier touches such as adding zips, badges or logos can gives clothes a more interesting look.

If you are not confident with your sewing skills, why not organise a clothes swapping party with some friends.

Why not visit your local charity shops, it is amazing what bargains you can find.

Take time to repair your clothes rather than just throwing them out.

Churchill, were reluctant to bring in clothes rationing, the Prime Minister rejecting the scheme more than once. In this, he misread the public mood, as he was generous enough to admit later to Oliver Lyttelton, the President of the Board of Trade. By now used to food rationing, people were ready, even happy, to accept clothes rationing, even if it meant going 'in rags and tatters on the bureaucratic orders of a minister', as Churchill had growled, because it meant fair shares for all.

In his wireless broadcast following the rationing announcement, former businessman Oliver Lyttelton said optimistically that he knew all the women of Britain would look smart, despite clothes rationing, 'but we men may look shabby. If we do we must not be ashamed. In war, the term "battle-stained" is an honourable one.' And, he went on, everyone

should remember, when they began to feel tired of their old clothes, 'that by making them do you are contributing some part of an aeroplane, a gun or a tank'.

Whatever else was true in his broadcast about clothes rationing, Mr Lyttelton was right about the different approach to clothes rationing taken by men and women. Throughout the war, 'looking her best' was promoted as the British woman's patriotic duty, while those men not in uniform on the whole made little of their increasingly shabby wardrobe.

The clothes rationing announcement was made on a Sunday. The next day, shops were crowded as people rushed to get in stocks of everything they thought they would need and which would soon be unavailable, or else might soon need more coupons than had been allocated. Many people managed to use up their

NO EXCEPTIONS
Even nurses and policewomen had to give up some of their precious clothing coupons to obtain parts of the uniform. Here a policewoman is guiding some evacuees to the train to take them to the safety of the country.

One saving grace of the new ration scheme, as far as women were concerned, was that hats were not included in it. Hats became the one area in wartime where women could really use their ingenuity to smarten up a plain outfit. Although turbans and hairnets became the headwear of choice for many women, especially those who worked in war factories, when it came to social occasions, women liked to wear a smart little hat.

On the whole, the clothes rationing system was better than that of food rationing, because the coupons could be used anywhere, rather than in one particular shop where you had to be a registered customer. Even so, the whole business, with its coupons, points and categories, became so complicated that the Board of Trade was forced to order the publication of a small booklet (price 2d) called *The Clothing Coupon Quiz* to help people find their way through the maze of rationing as it affected clothing, footwear and knitting yarn.

Another major problem with clothing rationing as it took hold was a sudden soaring in prices. Even if one had the right number of coupons, high prices – £42 for a suit that would have cost 14 guineas (£14.70) in 1939, or £12 for a 25-shilling (£1.25) nightdress – put many clothes beyond reach of the average man and woman. Eventually, the ever-watchful government stepped in.

A year after clothes rationing was imposed, the Board of Trade announced something new, which turned out to be something very welcome indeed. This was the Utility Clothing scheme, announced in a Civilian Clothing Order in June 1942. Utility clothing, like the Utility furniture that came after it, was a government-controlled way of ensuring that what clothing fabric there

allocation of coupons in one go, forgetting that there was a whole year to go before they would get any more. Women in uniformed jobs, such as nurses and policewomen, also had to remember that they would be obliged to give up some of their precious coupons for things like their nurse's dress or official-issue stockings.

THE VICTORY ROLL

In the late 1940s, the Victory Roll hairstyle was all the rage. It was both practical and neat, and allowed women to retain their femininity. This hairstyle is making a comeback and, although it is easy to replicate, you will need ample supplies of hairspray and plenty of bobby pins! Also, you have to remember that these were the days before hair dryers so women used to pin their wet hair into curls and sleep in them overnight so that their hair was easier to roll in the morning. The actresses Betty Grable and Rita Hayworth both used to wear their hair in the victory roll style.

- Decide where you want your parting – centre, side or extreme side – then part your hair and section it off behind each ear.
- Choose where you want to start your first roll. Hold this section of hair by the end and slowly roll it up, taking care to catch any stray hairs and adding them to the circle of hair as you go. Roll towards the centre of your head.
- When the circle of hair has reached your scalp, secure it next to your parting using bobby pins. Spray with plenty of hairspray to keep it in place.
- Repeat for the second curl and position so it is even with the first.

BETTY GRABLE
The actress Betty Grable was famous for wearing her hair in a victory roll.

was would be used to make well-designed, well-made, price-controlled clothes that would last instead of being wasted on over-priced, shoddily made clothing.

Top London couturiers, including Hardy Amies, Digby Morton and the Queen's dressmaker, Norman Hartnell, were asked to provide designs for four basic outfits, including top coats and suits for both men and women and two kinds of dress for women. The first 32 designs were shown in London in September 1942 and Utility clothing went on sale to the general public in Spring 1943, each item having

GOING TO THE RACES
When it came to social occasions women loved to wear a nice suit and a smart little hat, especially if they were going to the races.

a label with the Utility 'CC41' logo prominently displayed on it.

In the spirit of the times, Utility clothing had a pared-down, practical and almost military look about it. The Board of Trade was sternly practical in its instructions to designers and manufacturers, issuing a set of regulations rather grimly called 'Austerity'. Under Austerity regulations, men's suits were allowed narrow lapels only, and no turn-ups to the trousers, and women's clothes should be knee- not ankle-length and would be cut on severe lines. There would be a minimum number of buttons and definitely no unnecessary trimmings. Most people liked Utility clothing. As *Vogue* said, 'Now [everyone] will have an equal chance to buy beautifully designed clothes, suitable to their lives and incomes. It is

HOW CLOTHES RATIONING WORKED

Clothes rationing meant the distribution to everyone of ration coupons. Unlike food rationing at this time, the clothes rationing scheme involved from the beginning a points system in which every item of rationed clothing, including both outer garments and underwear, was given a points value. The greater the amount of material and labour that went into a garment, so its points value was higher.

In the first fifteen months of clothes rationing, everyone was given 66 coupons, with the first 26 of them coming in the form of the unused margarine coupons in the current food ration book. This was because the Board of Trade was so concerned to keep clothes rationing secret to prevent hoarding and the development of a black market, that it did not dare begin printing any clothing ration books.

The first clothing ration books, containing 60 coupons, appeared a year after clothing rationing was announced. There were three different coloured books, indicating that they contained coupons for different categories of people. These were intended to last until the end of July 1943, but everyone had to make do with the 60 coupons until September 1943, with the new books containing only 40 coupons, so insufficient had clothing textile production in Britain become. The 1944 books contained 48 coupons, but those issued in September 1945, when the war in Europe was over, had only 36 coupons. This, again, was because of the serious lack of workers in Britain's textile factories.

The Board of Trade, having done some secret research into the amounts and types of clothes that most people bought every year, thought that 66 coupons would be sufficient for the purchase of one complete outfit every year. With an overcoat for a man requiring 16 coupons and one for a woman taking 14 coupons, while a shirt needed 8 and a dress 11, this seemed optimistic. When the dress requirements of the changing seasons were taken into account, 66 coupons each for every man and woman not in uniform in the country began to sound very inadequate.

There were more generous allocations for workers in heavy industry, for expectant mothers, for babies and for older children, whose clothes required fewer coupons in acknowledgement of the fact that growing children quickly out-grew their clothes.

UTILITY CLOTHING
Four models show off the new utility fashions. The first and third from the left are wearing original West End fashions while the other two are wearing mass-produced outfits.

a revolutionary scheme and… an outstanding example of applied democracy'.

With new clothing now so severely rationed, taking care of the clothes that one owned became all the more important. In 1943 the Ministry of Information, acting on behalf of the Board of Trade, produced a smart little book, illustrated with neat, clear line drawings, called *Make Do and Mend*. In his Foreword, Hugh Dalton, President of the Board of Trade since early

1942, quickly thanked everyone for accepting clothes rationing so readily and repeated the by now well-worn phrases about saving 'much-needed shipping space, manpower and materials, and so assisting the war effort'. His main point was that the contents of the book had not been dreamed up in the dusty offices of the Board of Trade. Rather, they had been tested and approved by the Board's Make Do and Mend Advisory Panel, 'a body of practical people, mostly women'. Four of *Make Do and Mend*'s five chapters were concerned with the essential matter of clothes care. First, and most important, came a chapter on making clothes last much longer, by storing them properly, attending quickly to any necessary repairs, and dealing with moths before their grubs ate clothes material. Then came a lengthy chapter detailing the correct way to mend tears, darn holes, patch clothes, repair bindings, and carry out the many other kinds of repairs that clothing might need. This was followed by chapters on washing and cleaning clothes and on renovating them.

Last of all in *Make Do and Mend* came a chapter dealing with knitted woollen garments. While fabrics of all kinds – including furnishing fabrics, until the government forbad their use in clothing – were much in demand for the making of new clothes, almost as precious in the eyes of women was knitting wool, which was rationed. When, like everything else, new wool became an increasingly rare sight in the shops and on market stalls, women turned to the knitted sweaters that had been in their chests of drawers and ottomans for many years.

If a jumper, cardigan or pair of hand-knitted socks or gloves could not be repaired, smartened up, lengthened or shortened to suit another child in the family, then they could almost always be carefully unpicked, unravelled and knitted up again, perhaps together with other wools of the same weight but different colours: stripes

became a major design feature in wartime knitwear. One of the most important sections in *Make Do and Mend*'s knitwear chapter was the one telling the reader in detail how best to prepare and wash unravelled wool to make it ready for knitting up again.

The business of clothing oneself and one's family in wartime led very quickly to a new take on the 'make do and mend' and 'do-it yourself' habits of the 1930s. Current stocks of dress-making fabrics, indeed fabrics of all kinds, whether in shops, markets or stored away at home, became much sought-after, with stocks available to the public disappearing quickly.

Nella Last, visiting her local market in Barrow-in-Furness in May 1940 was delighted to find the 'job lot' stalls piled high with dresses, coats and shoes, many of them bearing the tags of a large Southport store. She bought a 'lovely piece of thick artificial crepe-de-chine for 1s 11d, because it was badly soiled from dropping on a dusty floor,' which she planned to use to make a blouse or a petticoat slip. Less than a year later, in March 1941, things were very different in the market, which had lost its joyous spirit. Now, Nella noted in her Mass Observation diary, 'grim-faced women queue and push – and hurry off to another queue when served. There is no beauty, or … leisureliness.… Round the remnant stalls there is a different crowd. There's no hunting from stall to stall for a bargain, to make a silk slip or blouse or "something to make our Willie a little overcoat".'

OPPOSITE: GET KNITTING

To make extra clothes for their children, mothers and grandmothers knitted jumpers and entire suits like the one this toddler is wearing, by unpicking old jumpers and other woollen items.

CLEVER WAYS WITH KNITWEAR

THRIFTY TIP

Here are some wartime suggestions for giving more wear time to old or badly worn knitwear:

• Give a new look to a jumper whose sleeves have become worn, particularly at the elbows, by cutting the sleeves off above the damaged section and binding the edges of the now short sleeves with a contrasting braid, ribbon or strip of fabric cut on the cross. Put the same binding round the jumper's neckline to complete the new look.

• Remove the sleeves from a plain-coloured jumper by unpicking them at the shoulder line. Knit new sleeves with a mixture of different coloured wools knitted in stripes or larger panels. Knit a pocket in the same pattern to sew on the jumper's front.

• A knitted garment that has shrunk or become matted can be carefully unpicked, first tacking over any unmatted sections so that the stitches do no run. Once unpicked, the various pieces of the garment can be used just like pieces of cloth and cut into shapes from a paper pattern. Matted wool cloth works well as boleros, waistcoats, children's coats, caps and even indoor slippers.

By the time the second clothing ration book was issued in 1943, a country-wide sub-culture of self-help and helping your neighbours had developed. 'Sew and Save' became as familiar a heading on all those government posters as 'Make Do and Mend'. Evening institutes, technical colleges and women's groups like the WVS and WI set up sewing and knitting classes to help those, women and men alike, who had never set a stitch or tried to knit anything, even a blanket square, in their lives. Children's clothing and shoe exchanges, many of them organised by the WVS, appeared in many towns. Local authorities opened advice centres where people could take their worn-out clothing and get advice on mending and renovating it.

At the neighbourhood level, women with sewing and knitting skills set up mending groups to help their neighbours and, ranging wider, to take in and repair the working clothes and overalls of local war workers. As the war went on and such basics as pins and needles and sewing threads became scarce, many women with sewing machines would hold sewing parties to which other women would bring their precious rag bags and piece-bags, even dressmakers' dummies, pooling their resources to make and renovate the clothes in their family's clothing cupboards and drawers.

With knitwear, especially, home knitting skills were used more widely than just for home and family use. Many a WVS or WI gathering was concerned with sharing out precious supplies of knitting wool so that thick sweaters, scarves and socks could be knitted for merchant seamen or Royal Navy men out in the cold North Atlantic – or even further afield.

PATTERN FOR 2-NEEDLE MITTENS

Approximate size for children not including the ribbed cuff:

Small – 5 inches long (1¾ in thumb)
Medium – 6 inches long (1¾ in thumb)
Large – 7½ inches long (2¼ in thumb)

Needles: Sizes 1.25 mm (18) and 1 mm (19)

- Cast on 34 sts.
- Rib in K2, P2, across. Continue ribbing for 20 rows. Last Row increasing to 38 sts, 4 sts evenly spaced.
- Change to larger needle and work in stocking stitch (st st) for 6 rows.
- Place marker between middle two stitches. (18 and 19th) add two stitches, then place another marker, Work in st st increasing 2 sts every other row between markers until you have 14 stitches. Put these 14 stitches on a holder for working the thumb later.
- Continue working in st st adding 2 stitches under the thumb once. Work in st st until total length of the mitten is 8.5 inches. (Or up to the top of pinky finger).
- Start decreasing as follows:
  Row 1: *K 2 tog, knit 8*, rep * across.
  Row 2 and all-even rows. Purl across even.
  Row 3: *K 2 tog, knit 7*, rep * across.
  Row 5: *K2 tog, knit 6*, rep * across.

Row 7: *K2 tog, knit 5*, rep * across.
Row 9: *K2 tog, knit 4*, rep * across.
Row 11: * K2 tog, knit 3*, rep * across.
Row 13: Knit 2 together across.

Weave yarn through stitches leaving a tail for sewing side seam later.

Thumb:
- Pick up the 14 stitch plus cast on an additional 2.
- Work the 16 stitches for 10 rows in st st.
- Next Row: knit 2 tog across the row.

Weave yarn through stitches and leave tail for sewing thumb seam.

HOW TO INCREASE:
Often seen as 'Inc' in patterns, the easiest way to make a stitch is by knitting in the front and the back of a stitch. First knit in the front of the stitch that needs to be increased but instead of sliding the right-hand needle to the front and taking the stitch off the left-hand needle, tilt the right hand needle so you can work a stitch in the back of the loop of the same stitch. Now you can slide the two new stitches off the left -hand needle and proceed as normal.

KNITTING FOR SOLDIERS
When the government asked people to start knitting for our armed forces overseas, people of all ages turned their hand to making socks, balaclavas and other much needed items.

As a government-issued poster reminded everyone, 'Our Jungle Fighters Want Socks – Please Knit Now', and there was space on the poster for a local council to add an address for obtaining information, patterns and wool.

The wartime emphasis on making do and mending, knitting and sewing, reached into all parts. School-children were given instruction in knitting and sewing, and even turning sheets, at school. Women – and a few men – knitted on buses and trains. Manufacturers turned their attention to providing such things as trouser-bottom protectors, replacement trouser pockets and patches for repairing damaged clothes. Professional launderers and dry-cleaners offered dyeing services, including dyeing garments to a lighter shade: 'Autumn frocks plus-dyed a lighter shade for Spring', advertised Clark's Dyers, offering to dye two frocks for 13/6 (approx 66p).

Like food and furniture rationing, clothing rationing did not end until well after the war.

As far back as January 1944, Hugh Dalton, President of the Board of Trade, warned that although he promised to do his best for civilians, he had to say that 'a continuance of clothes rationing, with modifications', would be necessary 'during the transition from war to peace'. Clothes rationing was not phased out in Britain until 1949.

The President of the Board of Trade might say more than once that to be shabby was actually to be patriotic, but the British people also made heroic efforts to be well-clothed and not too shabby during World War Wo. It was quite an achievement. Although the colours could be described as drab and the styles rather utilitarian, women still managed to look elegant and made accessories to enhance their outfits.

CLOTHES FOR CHILDREN

These war toddlers are being kitted out with warm winter clothes that have been kindly donated by the Americans at a depot in South West London.

RAIDING HUSBANDS' WARDROBES

The wardrobes of men away in the armed forces or too concerned with their wartime jobs to worry about their clothes, proved a valuable asset in the business of replenishing women's wartime wardrobes. Even the Board of Trade got in on this particular act by including a section called 'Men's Clothing into Women's' in its 1943 publication *Make Do and Mend*.

Particularly valuable targets were men's overcoats and jackets, with their splendid amounts of warm tweeds and woollen fabrics. 'A tweed jacket could be cut down to your own measurements and you could then wear it with a flannel skirt and a gay pullover,' recommended *Make Do and Mend*, blandly ignoring the fact that altering a heavy tailored garment required more than a little skill. Despite this, adapting men's coats and jackets to fit women was a common practice during the war.

The good quality black material in a man's dress suit was too good a wardrobe-replenishing opportunity to be missed, and many women made themselves expensive-looking, neat-fitting skirts from dress trousers and jackets from the jacket of a dress suit. The white shirts worn with dress suits could also, when unpicked and with the starch and dressing washed out of them, be re-made into smart women's shirts or children's clothes.

Rather easier was another renovating job tackled by many women: turning trousers into skirts. Even plus-fours could be unpicked and converted into skirts without too much trouble. There was usually enough fabric in a pair of plus-fours to make two pairs of boy's shorts.

As for worn silk ties – no woman with a plain dress to trim could ignore the fine fabric in these. Strips of silk tie could trim collars, cuffs and plackets of dresses and, if long enough, be turned into belts. And, of course, there was often a young son to be thought of. A worn tie, cut more narrowly and shorter would be ideal for a boy to wear on formal occasions.

Another male garment well suited to conversion was a heavy winter dressing-gown. Its shoulders taken in and worn with a leather belt to pull in its voluminous folds, a dressing-gown made a very good light-weight woman's casual coat.

THRIFTY TIP

WINNING THE WAR BY SAVING AND SALVAGING

What today's generation is learning to call recycling, and which we are doing to help 'save the planet', the wartime generation knew as 'salvaging', and did it to save the nation.

Throughout the war, the Ministry of Information, working on behalf of other ministries, notably those of Supply and Works but also the Board of Trade, operated a huge propaganda machine the main purpose of which was to persuade every man, woman and child in the country that it was their patriotic duty to save, economise on and salvage every scrap of material that could be used to help the war effort.

From the outset of the salvage campaign, the larger local authorities were legally required to organise the collection of salvage in their areas, with some of the responsibility for this soon being passed down the chain to smaller towns. Selling as much as possible of the material salvaged helped keep down local rates

Just as the Ministry of Food's 'Potato Pete' and 'Doctor Carrot' characters helped promote its food self-sufficiency propaganda and the Board of Trade's 'Mrs Sew-and-Sew' promoted

make-do-and-mend in the home, so the save and salvage propaganda campaign included two characters called 'Private Scrap' and the 'Squander Bug'. The former promoted good salvage, while the latter, an unpleasantly hairy, bug-shaped, swastika-wearing creature, featured as a sort of devil's advocate for Hitler promoting waste and the squandering of resources, especially money. In fact, the importance of the Squander Bug campaign lay in its message that simply not spending was the important thing.

While being as economical as possible with fuel and food were the main planks in the 'save and salvage' exercises of the war, there were also many other aspects of it that reached into almost every area of the average person's life. From pigswill bins in the streets and piles of saucepans from the nation's kitchens destined for Lord Beaverbrook's 'Spitfire fund' to waste paper gathered up by Boy Scouts, glassware, tins, leather, rubber (a Mae West lifejacket could be made from a pair of Wellington boots), electric bulbs and batteries and animal bones (good, the housewife was told, for fertiliser), there was little that could not be used in the fight, first for survival and then for victory.

As everything had value in the business of stretching scarce resources to their limits, it became second-nature in every household in the country to re-use or recycle almost everything, separating it into different boxes or bags, ready for taking to a collection point. Salvage was not just left to everyone to get on with in their own way, after one or two radio broadcasts from government ministers plus a few Ministry of Information adverts in newspapers and magazines. The official National Salvage scheme worked largely through such voluntary organisations as the Women's Voluntary Service (WVS), which organised salvage shops, dumps and collections points, not just in large towns but in remote villages.

The WVS and ARP wardens became the main organisers of salvage collection, with help from older children's organisations like the Boy Scouts and the Girl Guides, and also from the youth service organisations. Younger children also became an important cog in the salvage wheel – literally, since they were enrolled in corps of junior salvage collectors called 'Cogs', with their own *Cog Battle Song*, sung to the tune of *There'll Always be an England*:

> There'll always be a dustbin
> To save for victory
> So treat it right and let it fight
> For home and liberty
> We'll win this war together

SQUANDER BUG

DON'T TAKE THE SQUANDER BUG WHEN YOU GO SHOPPING

Here are some suggestions to help save our planet:

- Make short journeys by foot or bike, leave the car at home.
- Invest in a supermarket 'bag for life' to carry your shopping in.
- Use local recycling banks and services.
- Choose a shower over a bath to save water.
- Build a compost to recycle your kitchen waste.
- Use a washing line instead of the tumble drier when the weather is fine.
- Don't leave electrical appliances on standby, turn them off at the mains when not in use.

SALVAGE DEPOT
The WVS (Women's Voluntary Service) unload salvage at a depot where everything has to be sorted.

As easy as can be
If dustbins mean as much to you
As dustbins mean to me

Don't use it for your paper
Or fill it up with tins
For only dust, not bits of crust
Were meant to go in bins
We'll win this war together

As easy as can be
If dustbins mean as much to you
As dustbins mean to me

The oldest bits of cardboard
Can all be used again
It's quite well-known a cutlet bone
Will make an aeroplane
We'll win this war together

As easy as can be
If dustbins mean as much to you
As dustbins mean to me

The smallest piece of iron
Will turn into a gun
So save it now and show us how
The battle can be won
We'll win this war together
As easy as can be
If dustbins mean as much to you
As dustbins mean to me

Metal was a particularly important war material, and a scrap metal drive was launched as early as January 1940, during the Phoney War, with most reclaimed metal being taken by the Ministry of Works. There were two particularly famous metal salvage campaigns during the war: the Minister of Aircraft Production, Lord Beaverbrook's call for the collection of saucepans for Spitfires, and the compulsory dismantling and taking away of the iron railings round parks, gardens and houses, both of which were launched in 1940.

Lord Beaverbrook was a newspaper magnate who knew all there was to know about how to use newspapers to run a campaign. His manifesto, published in newspapers in July 1940 and given enormous impetus by a lunchtime broadcast appeal on 10 July from Lady Reading, head of the WVS, asked housewives to 'turn your pots and pans [and kettles, vacuum cleaners, hat pegs, coat hangers, cigarette boxes and much else] into Spitfires and Hurricanes, Blenheims and Wellingtons'. There was an immediate and extraordinary response from the public, who raided their kitchens to a

degree that as the war went on and metalware became increasingly difficult to buy, began to seem at best regrettable.

If the 'saucepans for Spitfires' campaign was ultimately a waste of saucepans – 'I suppose after the war they'll melt them down and make saucepans and things,' said the woman in a 1941 Punch cartoon watching Spitfires overhead – the campaign was a great success as a raiser of money for war planes. If a city, or group of people or even an individual, in Britain and in the countries of the Commonwealth, raised the £5000 said to be the price for a Spitfire, they could have one named after them.

As for the park railings campaign, most people liked it at the outset for it made parks and public gardens easily accessible, day and night – even though some local authorities continued to close plain wooden gates at night, just to make the point that this was a save and salvage scheme for the duration only. In reality, it was more than that; it was another indication that social equality was being brought nearer by the war and that the wealthy and privileged could no longer expect to cut themselves off from ordinary people behind high wrought-iron fences.

Waste paper was also a major theme of the save and salvage campaign. It was not just that paper was going to be scarce anyway because its manufacture used essential resources and occupied factory space, or else its importation took up valuable space in ships. But paper was itself a war material, used in the making of a wide range of things, from the wing-tips of gliders to the heating pipes in a bomber. Boys Scouts became the nation's leading collectors of waste paper. Virginia Woolf thought it worth mentioning in her diary in May 1940

PRECIOUS RUBBISH
Pupils of Burghley Road School, near St Pancras Station, London, bring their salvage contributions of old newspapers, cardboard boxes etc, to a lorry touring the borough.

that she had been interrupted in her writing by the jangling of the door bell and by the now familiar cry of 'Any waste paper' from a small boy in white sweater, come, she supposed, for the Scouts.

When *Good Housekeeping* ran a Paper Salvage competition, offering prizes for the best suggestions for both collecting paper and for finding useful substitutes for it, they had a large response. The many suggestions ranged from the fairly obvious: keep a designated bag or box in the house into which every scrap of paper (don't forget those bus tickets) and cardboard should be put, and use fir cones, twigs, dried bracken, leaves and garden rubbish instead of paper to light the fire, to the ingenious: save

THE VALUE OF BONES

By 1944 many people, viewing the salvage dumps piled high with old tyres and rubber boots, rusted iron, leather boots and shoes, rags and bones that littered many an open space in town and country, were beginning to feel that perhaps they had done enough on the save and salvage front. And as for that bin or basket of bones kept just inside the front gate, so that it would not be tripped over in the blackout, it was a target for every dog in the neighbourhood and smelled badly in summertime.

A timely newspaper advert from Imperial Chemical Industries (ICI) aimed at keeping everyone up to the saving mark by homing in on bones as a good example of the magic that the chemist could perform to make 'new forms arise from the scrap-heap like the Phoenix from its own ashes'.

HOW YOUR SALVAGE HELPS TO MAKE A RESCUE LAUNCH

1 SCRAP METAL SCRAP IRON NEEDED FOR STEEL HULL. STEEL NEEDED FOR MAKING ENGINE AND MACHINE-GUNS. BRASS MAKES CARTRIDGE CASES. 3-PINT TIN KETTLE MAKES 40 MACHINE-GUN BULLETS. PHOSPHOR BRONZE NEEDED FOR PROPELLOR. COPPER FOR RADIO COMPONENTS

2 ROPE, STRING, TWINE MAKE NEW SHIPS ROPE

3 WASTE PAPER ONE ENVELOPE MAKES 50 WADS FOR MACHINE GUN CARTRIDGES. TWELVE OLD LETTERS MAKE A CAR-TRIDGE BOX. WASTE PAPER ALSO MAKES GAS-KET WASHERS FOR ENGINE AND PROVIDES INSULATION FOR RADIO

4 SCRAP RUBBER MAKES ELECTRICAL AND RADIO INSULATORS AND COMPONENTS

5 BONES GIVE GLYCERINE—A COM-PONENT IN CORDITE CHARGES FOR MACHINE-GUN CARTRIDGES

6 RAGS COTTON RAGS MAKE SPECIAL GRADES OF PAPER FOR CHARTS ALSO ENGINE WIPERS

First, [bones] are treated with solvents to remove the fats from which is made glycerine. Glycerine treated with acids becomes an explosive, nitro-glycerine from which is made cordite.
The degreased bones are then steamed to yield glue and gelatine which, with glycerine, go to produce a wide range of articles from printing rollers to adhesives.

What then remains of the bones may be ground into a fertiliser or feeding stuff, or heated in steel retorts to extract bone oil from which many drugs are made.

All that is now left is a charcoal called bone black… even this is used in sugar refining and when spent, may be burned into bone ash and [used] in the manufacture of china, or as an assay for gold and silver!

All this from the chicken, beef and lamb bones taken from the kitchen and tossed into the bones bin or basket in the street.

REUSING FAT

Even today used cooking oils and fats can be recycled into biofuels. These biofuels burn much cleaner than other forms of petrol or diesel and are therefore much kinder to the environment. New biofuel technology has been developed by engineers that turns any fat source – vegetable, animal fat and even oils from algae – into a high-powered fuel for jet engines.

envelopes by folding letters neatly and sealing the edges with the sticky paper from the edges of stamps, and use a coat of paint, American cloth or Cellophane rather than paper to line drawers, or just leave them bare.

The non-availability of writing paper became a major annoyance in an age when the only way to communicate with a father, son or daughter or husband serving overseas was to write to them. Even W. H. Smith, one of the nation's leading stationers, was forced to confess in its advertising in 1942 that it could still offer a 'fair' choice of writing papers – in other words, a small, limited amount – so the company advised its customers in distinctly nannying terms to use it carefully, fill both sides of each sheet of paper, and to write small in close-spaced lines. As Messrs Smith said, it wasn't just a matter of making a little go a long way. 'Paper makes MUNITIONS so please don't forget to out for salvage every scrap of old paper and cardboard in the house.'

Saving money for the nation, such as by buying Defence Bonds instead of a new hat or some other treat, was a major thread in Britain's save and salvage approach to winning the war. The National Savings campaign spent huge sums of money during the war exhorting everyone to contribute to the war effort by putting their money, not into consumer goods, but into some form of National Savings. There were large advertising campaigns, many of them aimed at readers of women's magazines, propaganda films intended for showing in cinemas and even a *Weekly Savings News* programme broadcast on the BBC every Sunday evening, carefully timed to follow the 6 o'clock news broadcast, when most people were sitting round their wireless sets getting

WAYS OF USING OLD PAPER

As this old American poster told us during the war 'Paper packs a punch, save waste paper!' There are many uses for old newspapers, so before you throw them in the dustbin why not consider some of these alternatives.

• Use old newspapers to make an unusual wrapping paper, you can always add things like a bright bow or a piece of ribbon.

• Crumple up balls of old newspaper and stuff them into the toes of your trainers to remove nasty niffs!

• Use crumpled up newspaper to give a final buff when you next clean your windows. See how your glass sparkles.

• Use several sheets of newspaper to protect the carpets in your car from mud and dirt.

• Wrap green tomatoes in sheets of newspaper and layer them in a box. Close the lid and check every few days until the tomatoes have ripened to a rosy red.

• Place a sheet of newspaper in the base of your vegetable drawer in the fridge. Not only will it absorb odours but it will also stop it getting messy from rotted produce.

• Roll up newspapers and tie them tightly with string. Use them in your fireplace as an alternative to logs.

• Use newspapers as mulch in your fruit, vegetable and flower garden. Alternatively cut a hole in the middle of each sheet and slide it over the plant to help keep weeds at bay and moisture in.

• When sending fragile items by post, shred up some newspaper as protection.

ANY OLD IRON
All available scrap metal was needed to make munitions and these men are removing the iron railings from Spencer Parade in Northampton as part of a salvage scheme.

the latest news on the progress of the war. The National Saving Movement's War Savings Campaign eventually had nearly twelve thousand local committees promoting the work of the hundreds of thousands of individual savings groups that were soon set up in offices, factories, schools, ARP posts and many other places. The groups in schools enabled pupils to buy National Savings Stamps, which they put into a special savings book. The main task of all these groups was to encourage the thrifty use of money, ideally by either saving it in one of the Movement's savings schemes, or putting it into special savings drives promoted by local savings groups from as early in the war as 1941, by which time the threat of invasion had almost disappeared.

These 'savings drives', which usually ran

HOW TO BE A PAPER BAG SQUANDER BUG

Becoming a squander bug, and thus forcing a ship to make what the stern editor of *Everywoman* magazine dramatically referred to as 'a perilous journey on the high seas to fetch… paper' involved holding on to rather than putting in the salvage box old bills, letters, newspapers and magazines that had been read, wrapping paper and cardboard boxes, even bus tickets and shop receipts. Destroying them at home was even worse, said the *Everywoman* editor: this was destroying the means of making British weapons as surely as if the householder had helped blow up a munitions dump.

This high-flown rhetoric illustrated a view of save and salvage that took on what could have become a distinctly anti-culture tone if it had been let get out of hand. Old books, in contrast to books printed on War Economy Standard paper, began to look like valuable stocks of high-quality material, rather than books in their own right, while their owners were being turned into Squander Bugs by keeping them on their bookshelves.

In 1943 the Ministry of Supply promoted book drives that had brought in 56 million books by October. Only six million of these were spared by scrutiny committees which, having set aside very valuable books, used the remainder to replenish library stocks and to provide the armed services with reading material. The other fifty million books were pulped to make paper for new books.

for a week in each locality, but which could be organised up and down the country for months on end, were given patriotic themes. There were War Weapons Weeks in 1941, Warship Weeks in 1942, Wings for Victory Weeks throughout the spring and summer of 1943, and Salute the Soldier Weeks in 1944. If the Week was being held in a large town or city, it was usually accompanied by parades, speeches from local leaders and service officers on leave, and exhibitions highlighting the uses for the money raised. Although there were people, mostly financiers and economists, but also ordinary citizens who felt, like Virginia Woolf's friend Lady Oxford, that there was no virtue in saving, but much more in spending because spending – that is, consuming – helped the economy to keep moving; economic historians see things rather differently. On the whole, they agree that there was a real economic value to the wartime savings schemes, because the diversion of private spending into savings had a valuable anti-inflationary effect.

While there was an important morale-boosting thread in the government's 'save and salvage' propaganda which said that by

HOW TO SAVE

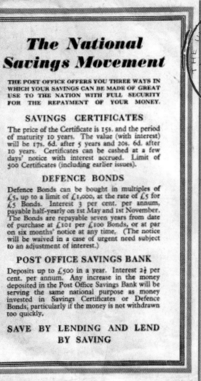

The National Savings Movement

THE POST OFFICE OFFERS YOU THREE WAYS IN WHICH YOUR SAVINGS CAN BE MADE OF GREAT USE TO THE NATION WITH FULL SECURITY FOR THE REPAYMENT OF YOUR MONEY.

SAVINGS CERTIFICATES

The price of the Certificate is 15s. and the period of maturity 10 years. The value (with interest) will be 17s. 6d. after 5 years and 20s. 6d. after 10 years. Certificates can be cashed at a few days' notice with interest accrued. Limit of 500 Certificates (including earlier issues).

DEFENCE BONDS

Defence Bonds can be bought in multiples of £5, up to a limit of £1,000, at the rate of £5 for £5 Bonds. Interest 3 per cent. per annum, payable half-yearly on 1st May and 1st November. The Bonds are repayable seven years from date of purchase at £101 per £100 Bonds, or at par on six months' notice at any time. (The notice will be waived in a case of urgent need subject to an adjustment of interest.)

POST OFFICE SAVINGS BANK

Deposits up to £500 in a year. Interest 2½ per cent. per annum. Any increase in the money deposited in the Post Office Savings Bank will be serving the same national purpose as money invested in Savings Certificates or Defence Bonds, particularly if the money is not withdrawn too quickly.

SAVE BY LENDING AND LEND BY SAVING

Money was scarce during the war and there were restrictions on everything. Today people tend to spend beyond their means. The frugal wartime housewife would probably be horrified at the huge sums of money we spend on eating out, clothes and luxury gadgets. She would suggest you save money by growing your own vegetables and replacing clothes or furniture by becoming skilled at sewing or DIY.

But for those less likely to take this approach, simply being careful with your money could help you from going into serious debt.

- Make a list of your monthly outgoings – rent/mortgage, household bills, loan payments etc. Work out how much is left after you have paid all your bills and decide on a reasonable amount you could put into, say, an ISA each month.

- Unless you can afford to pay your credit card off each month, don't be tempted to get one.

- Plan your meals in advance and always take a shopping list with you so that you are not tempted to buy anything extra.

- Never go food shopping when you are hungry as you will be tempted to let your stomach rule your head!

- Walk more and drive less. You will be amazed how much money you will save on petrol and you will be getting fit at the same time so no need for expensive gym memberships.

FEEDING THE PIGS

Two women put their food scraps in a bin, aiding a scheme set up in Cheltenham, where bins were distributed around the town for people to get rid of their leftovers. This provided twenty tons of pig food weekly.

'saving and salvaging', everybody could take pride in knowing that they were doing their bit and making a direct contribution to fighting the war and that they were being active fighters on the Home Front, there was also a rather sternly puritanical note to this appeal of public patriotism. 'Let Your Conscience Be Your Guide' said the notice over the line of waste bins, separately labelled for pig food, bones, tins and paper, set up in a street in Cheltenham.

This stern undertone could be seen in action in the hundreds of thousands of people who were prosecuted in the courts and fined during the war for what sound today to be relatively minor infringements of many of the economy and saving regulations and orders promulgated in wartime. Many women were fined for rushing off to work leaving lights on in the house, thus not only infringing the blackout rules but also wasting fuel. A woman was fined for allowing

NATIONAL SAVINGS CERTIFICATES

N ational Savings Certificates, which everyone could buy – even, according to a typical National Savings propaganda film, small boys finding a few coins in a forgotten piggy bank – were launched in November 1939. The first National Savings Certificate was worth 15 shillings (75 pence) and would have a value of 17 shillings and 6 pence after five years, and £1 and 6 pence after ten years.

The certificates were exempt from income tax, and the government therefore decided that people could only hold a maximum of five hundred National Savings Certificates. This was fine for people on small incomes or fixed wages (and for children with piggy banks topped up by relatives), but people with a little more disposable income might be looking for more. For them, the National Savings scheme offered at the same time as the Savings Certificates a new Three Per Cent Defence Bond, costing £5, and purchasable in multiples of £5, with a maximum holding of £1000.

And what were the benefits of holding these savings certificates and bonds? Well, for a start, said a typical National Savings advert in 1940, Jill, buying her savings certificates in the Post Office, was supporting Jack away in the Navy. 'Jill's the girl! She'll never let it be said that the boys who are risking their lives for us were let down because people at home could not make sacrifices.... Some day [Jill's] savings may help to start a home – meanwhile they're helping to win the War!'

her maid to put stale bread, which could have been used in cooking, out on the bird table. Then there was the woman who carefully banked up her fire before she went out, only to arrive home later than intended so that the fire was burning away merrily again and an ARP warden saw it through her window. She was fined because of the blackout regulations, but was also told that her behaviour, in allowing her fire to warm an empty house, was selfish in the extreme.

This rather dark side aside, there is no doubt that on the whole the great wartime save and salvage campaign made a worthwhile contribution to the war effort, enabling every man, woman and child in the country to do his and her bit on a generous scale.